Preach the Word

Overseas Missionary Fellowship
1058 Avenue Road
Toronto, Ontario M5N 2C6

PREACH THE WORD
Denis Lane

 EVANGELICAL PRESS

EVANGELICAL PRESS
P.O. Box 5, Welwyn, Hertfordshire AL6 9NU, England

© *Overseas Missionary Fellowship Publishers, 1976*

First Evangelical Press edition 1979

ISBN 0 85234 137 7

All quotations from Scripture used in this book are taken from the Revised Standard Version.

Cover design by Peter Wagstaff

Printed in England by Biddles Ltd., Guildford.

Contents

Preface

'Tomorrow is already here and we are all set for yester-day.' I do not know the author of this pithy sentence, but when I first read it the message came through clearly. But is this really what is wrong with the church of God today? That by and large we are ineffective is too plain for argument, but why are we Christians generally so weak? Are we simply out of date? Can we remedy the defect by getting 'with it' or do our problems go much deeper? I believe they do.

Hosea described the problems of his day in terms of lack of knowledge. Ignorance of truth led to ineffective-ness of life. Worse than that, lack of knowledge of God produced a lack of morality as plain as what appears on the pages of any modern newspaper. 'There is no faith-fulness or kindness and no knowledge of God in the land' moaned Hosea, but 'there is swearing, lying, killing, stealing and committing adultery. . . therefore the land mourns' (Hos. 4:1,2). Men who have little grasp of truth and little knowledge of God have little hope of stability in their society. Hosea's diagnosis proved true for his day and proves true of ours.

But how many Christians really know what their faith is all about? How many can give a reason for their beliefs? How many see Christian truth as a whole where individual truths fit into the picture?

The prophet carried his diagnosis further and deeper.

He did not blame the people but their teachers. 'With you is my contention, O priest. . . . My people are destroyed for lack of knowledge' (Hos. 4:4,6). The priests who should have been their teachers had rejected knowledge and forgotten the law of their God. Lack of knowledge among the people of God meant a lack of teaching by the servants of God. In Hosea's day the lack of teaching could be traced to refusal to accept the true source of knowledge in God's law. Therefore it is not surprising that today, in churches where men think they know better than to take the Word of God at its face value, there is little understanding of spiritual truth. The real tragedy is, however, that in churches where the Word of God is fully believed and accepted, still the people starve for lack of instruction. Preaching there is in plenty, but little consecutive teaching and not too much result in changed lives. The famine of 'hearing the words of the Lord' described by Amos in 8:11,12 is only accentuated by the gladness with which the exposition of the Scriptures is welcomed where it can be found.

I speak as a preacher and pastor myself. Why do our people starve in the midst of plenty? I firmly believe that it is because too often we indulge in 'blessed thoughts' and too infrequently teach the Word of God in all its fulness. We take our thoughts and hang them onto Scripture instead of allowing the Scriptures to control our thoughts. We use a text as a kind of launching platform to be left behind after take-off and we never return to it. Then we say what is from our own hearts, and this may have no foundation at all in the text itself. Sincere exhortation and a fund of good stories, however, are no substitute for the convincing power and authority of the Word of God.

Often we do not realize just how little of our preaching is exposition of what the Word of God actually says. We may think we are expounding, when in fact we are not. A simple test will show us whether our preaching and teaching are expository or not. Do our hearers feel compelled to open their Bibles and do they refer to them when we are speaking? Or have they become so accustomed to our 'blessed thoughts' that their Bibles sit closed in front of them, or worse still, lie neglected at home?

Today we are seeing a welcome return to a more biblical way of church life where the ordinary Christian can play his full part, yet, wherever men expound the Word of God in the power of the Spirit, hearts warm to the truth and lives are changed. My prayer is that God might use this small book to help others to increase their effectiveness in proclaiming the Word of God in power.

D. J. V. Lane

Singapore

1

The preacher and his message

Truth through personality

God has chosen to pass His message through men. His supreme revelation of Himself came to us in a Man, the Word made flesh. In Jesus Christ truth had a perfect human medium through which to reach us. The rays of true light were not bent, darkened or hindered by passing through the transparent personality of the Lord.

Despite our failings, God still chooses to bring truth to men through other men. Philip Brooks in his famous *Lectures on Preaching* describes preaching as 'truth mediated through personality'. 'God,' says Paul in 2 Corinthians 5:20, is 'making his appeal through us' in our position as ambassadors for Christ. Effective preaching depends on much more than good speaking, careful construction of the message and knowledge of methods. What we *are* determines the kind of message our hearers receive. Our personality and personal relationship with God are vital parts of our preaching. We cannot live carelessly from Monday to Saturday and expect to preach with power on Sunday.

Jeremiah's call and ministry underline the importance God attaches to the person of the speaker. God knew him before he was born, consecrated and appointed him a prophet before Jeremiah himself could walk around the room (Jer. 1:4). He had no choice about his work and his objections on account of his age were brushed aside by the command to go to the people God wanted to speak to, with the message they needed to hear (Jer. 1:7). Jeremiah was to speak and the result would be God's words in his human mouth, truth mediated through personality (Jer. 1:9). The authority thereby given to Jeremiah's position is repeated again and again in Scripture with men like Moses, Samuel, Elijah, Isaiah and Daniel. God's ways do not change. God's method is still men.

What greater privilege, then, can any of us have than to be called of God to be His messenger to our own people today? Yet how few are happy to accept this calling for themselves or their children, if the door to medicine or law or some other well-paid profession remains open!

God's plan

Let us look more closely at the preacher and his own position in God's plan for bringing truth to men. John the Baptist pointed his generation towards Christ. His ministry is described in Mark 1:2: 'Behold I send my messenger before thy face, who shall prepare thy way.'

1. His command

Firstly, the only justification for preaching is the God-given confidence that God has said, 'Behold, I send you' (cf. Ezek. 2:3,4). This command cannot be refused. When God sends we must obey, whatever our plans, however good our education, whatever our family thinks. If God does not send, we dare not go. When God sends we must go (1 Cor. 9:16,17). The church needs men of God in the ministry. Why then are so few coming forward, especially from the ranks of university graduates? Does God not call or are some people not listening?

2. His messenger

Secondly, John the Baptist is described as 'my messenger' and in these two words lie both the glory and the humility of the preacher. To be the messenger of the living God, the Creator of the universe, is as high a privilege as can ever be given to a man. Yet at the same time to be a messenger is to be given a humble position of responsibility. A messenger is a nobody, sent by somebody with a communication. His responsibility rests in passing on the message. He is not important, and his only privilege lies in the person who sent him. The messenger does not construct the message; he only delivers it. He must not change it or give it his own meaning. He is the servant not only of the one who sent him, but also of the message with which he is sent.

3. His forerunner

Thirdly, in the case of the preacher, the messenger has the particular responsibility of 'preparing thy way' or 'preparing the way of the Lord'. He goes in front to prepare his hearers for Someone vastly more important who Himself intends to come. The preacher's job consists of delivering the message and then getting out of the way. 'He must increase, but I must decrease' could well be set over every place where men preach. Sometimes I feel like crying out to the preacher in the middle of his message, 'Get out of the way, man, get out of the way.' He comes across well, but his Lord remains hidden in the messenger's shadow.

The same combination of privilege and responsibility, of glory and humility appears again and again in Scrip-

ture. A particularly clear passage is 2 Corinthians 5:20
which may be set out as follows:

We are ambassadors for Christ	representing the God who called us
God making His appeal	the divine authority of preaching
through us	the human personality of the messenger
we beseech you	the human personality of the messenger
on behalf of Christ	the divine authority
Be reconciled to God	the message.

From the above, the preacher clearly occupies a place
of particular privilege and special responsibility. He has
a high office to occupy and a humble service to give.
What then should be the marks of those of us called to
be preachers of the Word of God? We will look at these
marks in relation to God, to the message and to the
hearers.

Marks of an expository preacher

1. A sense of the greatness and reality of God

Unless we *feel* with our hearts as well as *know* with our
minds the reality and greatness of the living God, our
message will carry no conviction. Isaiah needed to see
the Lord high and lifted up, reigning, worshipped, His
glory filling the earth, before he could begin his ministry
(Isa. 6:1-8). Ezekiel saw God, unknowable yet self-
revealing, always moving yet never changing, self-consist-
ent, reigning over all, holy yet merciful (Ezek. 1).
Daniel's strength drained from him as he fell on his face

before the reality that is God (Dan. 10:2-9). John the apostle fell at the feet of the risen Christ like a dead man when the vision burst upon him (Rev. 1:12-17). Even the Lord Himself spent forty days and nights alone submitting Himself to His Father's will before beginning His ministry. 'Listen to men who listen to God,' A.W. Tozer advised Christians. Part of our poverty in preaching today is poverty in our knowledge of God.

2. A sense of helplessness apart from God's enabling

Isaiah saw the Lord Himself dealing with the problem of his unclean lips. Ezekiel was told to stand on his feet and was given the Spirit to enable him to do so. The Lord put His hand on Daniel and set him at first on trembling hands and knees and then in a fully upright position. John was told not to fear, as the Lord's right hand touched his prostrate body. The man who has known the greatness and reality of God does not speak lightly or quickly. He knows in truth as well as in theory that without Christ we can do nothing (John 15:5). The world chatters on today, but few men speak from the presence of God in a conscious dependence on His power. Our world is full of words but knows little of the Word that comes from God. We cannot bring others that Word without taking the time to listen to what God has to say to us first.

3. Responsibility to make the message a part of himself

When Ezekiel was commissioned to preach he was told to open his mouth and to eat what God gave him (Ezek. 2:8). He then saw the message written out before him on a scroll, and it was anything but pleasant. The scroll was filled with words of 'lamentation and mourning and woe', and no man is anxious to proclaim such a message.

He was warned, however, to eat the scroll, to 'fill his stomach with it' and to 'go, speak to the house of Israel'. When he obeyed, the taste of the Word of God, despite its unpleasant message, was sweet as honey to his mouth. Clearly as a preacher he was to receive it into his own heart, to hear it with his own ears, and to make it thoroughly a part of himself before he went to speak to other people. In the same way, the apostle John in his first Epistle (1 John 1:1-3) commended the truth to men. This truth was 'the word of life'. He could commend this Word because he had heard, seen, looked upon and touched it for himself. The message came from his heart and personal experience. Likewise in Isaiah 50:4-5 the prophet had 'the tongue of those who are taught', and he knew how 'to sustain with a word him that is weary'. What preacher would not covet such an ability in his ministry? Isaiah gained that ability because morning by morning God had wakened him to hear as one who is taught, and he had been ready to respond despite the suffering and shame involved (vv. 5,6). As George Adam Smith says, 'The prophet learns his speech as the little child by listening. Grace is poured upon the lips through the open ear.' Significantly this passage is a prophecy of Christ Himself. The morning-by-morning listening of the preacher to the voice of God should be a fruitful source of material for ministry to others, but it is a demanding task.

4. Courage to express what he has received from God.

Jeremiah was warned not to decry his youthfulness (Jer. 1:6-8), nor to be dismayed by reactions to his preaching (Jer. 1:17-19). His hearers would fight against him, but his God would make him a fortified city, and would be there to deliver him. Ezekiel was told that if he had

gone to a people of a foreign language they would have
listened to him, but his own people were hard-headed
and stubborn-hearted. God promised to harden Ezekiel's
head more than theirs, though he never spoke of harden-
ing his heart (Ezek. 2:5-11). The youthful Samuel was
warned by the aged Eli not to keep to himself a message
God had given him for others (1 Sam. 3:17,18).

5. Willingness to learn and obey God's Word

In relation to his hearers the preacher must sit under the
Word of God with them. His position in the pulpit does
not place him above the Word because God may have as
much to say to him as to his hearers. Paul told Timothy
to command and teach these things in 1 Timothy 4:11.
'These things' were actually commands already given to
Timothy himself in the preceding verses. He was to be
'nourished on the words of the faith and of the good
doctrine which you followed'. He was to 'have nothing
to do with godless and silly myths', and so on.

6. Concern to understand and meet the hearers' needs

Some preachers rarely visit their congregations. How can
they understand people whom they do not know? The
Word of God does not change from generation to generation, but it does need to be freshly applied to the hearts
and minds of men in terms which they can understand.
Ezekiel had to go and sit among the exiles himself
before he could begin his ministry (Ezek. 3:15) and he
found it an overwhelming experience. Moses endured
forty years of the wilderness before God called him to
lead the people of Israel through the same blistering
desert. The Lord Himself was able to preach to
publicans and sinners because He thoroughly understood
them. How essential therefore for the preacher to have

regular up-to-date contact with the men to whom he
ministers, in their thoughts, hopes, fears and desires. He
is not to accommodate the gospel to them to make it
more popular, but he must be able to apply the gospel
to their needs in terms that are relevant to them. Jesus'
illustrations were drawn from everyday life. They spoke
to the heart.

I have spent considerable space on the place of the
preacher for this is the key to effective preaching. The
Lord Jesus Christ had the most effective ministry of all
because, on the one hand, He was in the closest living
contact with His Father, and on the other, He was in
continuous vital contact with ordinary men. When He
spoke, He spoke in the name and from the presence of
the living God. He also spoke to the needs of the men of
His own day so that they went away with lasting
impressions of the authority of His teaching (Mark 1:22)
and the depth of His understanding. If we would be
effective preachers and teachers of the Word we must
listen to God and understand men. For the preacher this
involves the tension between the study and the street,
between pulpit preaching and pastoral visiting. Both are
essential to a truly effective ministry.

Study questions

1. Make a study of one or all of the following passages:
   Isaiah 6, Jeremiah 1, Ezekiel 1—3:27, Daniel 10,
   Revelation 1:9-20.
   Note down especially:
   a. How the person saw and experienced God;
   b. the relation between his particular vision and the
      needs of the people of his day;
   c. how the preacher felt about himself;

    d. how God made the preacher feel able to do his work;

    e. the qualities required of the preacher;

    f. the content and limitations of his message.

2. How did each of these preachers identify with their people?

3. What things in the personal lives and histories of these preachers did God use to fit them for their ministry?

4. How can we develop our knowledge and vision of God?

2

The nature of expository preaching

When we speak of expository preaching, what do we really mean? Most preaching begins with a biblical text, so there is obviously more to it than that.

Old Testament background

The best way to understand true exposition is to look at the nature of preaching in the Scriptures. An example is in the book of Nehemiah 8:1-8.

1. Eager listeners

The first thing we notice here is the background to the preaching. Verse 1 speaks of all the people gathering as one man into the square before the Water Gate and of their telling Ezra the scribe to bring the Book of the Law of Moses 'which the Lord had given to Israel'. Here was a people united in their desire to hear the Word of God and recognizing the Book of the Law of Moses not simply as the writing of one of their patriarchs but as the gift of God to His people. They wanted to hear what God had to say to them. They were an extremely eager congregation, for Ezra read from the book from early morning until midday and they were all ears to hear him. Happy is the preacher who has a congregation hungry for the Word of God, as opposed to the man whose elders or deacons or council make it clear that ten minutes is all that they can stand.

2. Submission

The gathering was not held in the temple or any other special building, but Ezra the scribe stood on a wooden pulpit so that when he spoke to them 'he was above all the people'. When he opened the book the people stood and the impression given is that they stood for the whole of the discourse. Many people object today to the symbolism of the pulpit above the congregation, forgetting that the symbol is not that of the preacher's infallibility but of the people's submission to the Word of God. There was strong unity on this occasion also, and Ezra's fellow leaders stood with him, thereby emphasizing their united acceptance of the authority of the Law.

3. Worship

Before Ezra began to expound the Word of God 'he blessed the Lord, the great God; and all the people answered, 'Amen, Amen,' lifting up their hands; and they bowed their heads and worshipped the Lord with their faces to the ground.' While there is no reason why the ministry of the Word of God has to take place at the same time in the service each week, there is good scriptural reason for preparing the heart to receive the Word through worship. As any preacher knows, the quality of the worship in the church makes his task easier or harder.

So much for the background. What we are mainly interested in is the example of good exposition that verse 8 clearly describes for us. Really it is quite simple. First of all they read from the book, which all of them recognized as the law of God. In modern times we not only hear the Word read but can read and follow for

ourselves in our own Bibles. They did not have copies of
their own. Having read from the book, 'they gave the
sense, so that the people understood the reading'. There
was more to this than making the people understand the
actual words that were being read. They needed to
understand the sense, that is, they needed to know what
that particular part of the Word of God had to say to
them in their day and in their circumstances. Only then
could the people take the Word away with them and put
it into practice.

A definition

Exposition of the Scripture, therefore, is that process
whereby the meaning of a particular passage in the Bible
is so explained in terms of the needs and circumstances
of the congregation, that the people understand what
God is saying to them. An essential part of exposition
must then be to draw a parallel between the circumstances when the passage was written and the circumstances existing today, so that the principles of the
Word of God that never change can be interpreted in the
light of present needs. In Ezra's day, not only did the
people understand the reading but the exposition was
soon translated into action. Preaching that does not
cause that to happen is of little value.

The preaching had an emotional result and in verse 9
the people began to weep. The hearts of the people were
stirred. We must not be afraid to move people deeply. In
verses 10-12 the immediate result was sharing and
rejoicing, and in verse 13 and the following verses the
end result was action in obedience to the will of God.
True biblical exposition is not meant just to interest the
minds of men, but to influence their wills to action. The
process involves informing the mind, but also moving

the heart and stirring the will.

New Testament examples

We now turn to some examples of exposition in the New Testament. They are not in the strict context of preaching, but none the less show clearly the basic principles of exposition.

The Master Translator

Both come in Luke 24 and both come from the Lord Jesus Christ Himself. On the road to Emmaus we read that, 'Beginning with Moses and all the prophets, he interpreted to them in all the Scriptures the things concerning himself.' He interpreted the Scriptures for them and Luke uses a word for interpretation which in Acts 9:36 is expressed as 'translate'. Translation is the process by which language not immediately understood by the hearer is made understandable. We are familiar with this in ordinary life. The process of exposition does just this for the Scriptures. The job of the preacher is to take language which may be hard to understand because of lack of knowledge of background circumstances, history or other reasons and to give the language meaning in terms that everyone can understand.

The Master Expositor

You will notice also that Jesus began with Moses and the prophets. He used the Old Testament. That was all He had, but it was enough. The two on the road to Emmaus could not understand how it was that Christ should suffer and die. Jesus took the Old Testament and showed them from place after place how God had said that it would happen that way. We often find the Old Testament difficult. In fact, if we are honest, most of us

rarely preach from it. The customs and culture and
history of Israel seem so far removed from twentieth-
century life. Yet basically man has not changed. He still
loves and fears, hates and hopes as he did in those days
of Scripture. What is needed is for someone to translate
the lasting principles of action into terms that relate to
the life of modern man. That is the job of the preacher.
Just as the Lord Jesus could take the whole sweep of
the Old Testament and show them 'the things concerning Himself', so we should be able to see Christ there
and explain Him to our hearers. Jesus' message that day
was a Scripture-based, Christ-centred explanation that
left their hearts burning within them. True exposition
does just that.

In verse 44 of the same chapter we have another illustration of exposition. This time the text was taken from
the Lord's own words. 'These are my words which I
spoke to you while I was still with you.' He then went
on to show that these words which He had spoken were
in accordance with the words written about Him in the
Law, the Prophets and the Psalms; in other words in all
three major divisions of the Hebrew Scriptures. In verses
45-47 the Lord then 'opened their minds to understand
the Scriptures'; this was exposition. The word for
opening their minds is one that means to open completely or thoroughly, and is used elsewhere of opening the eyes of the blind, of Stephen's seeing heaven
opened (Acts 7:56), of the Lord's opening Lydia's heart
(Acts 16:14) and again of Jesus' opening to them the
Scriptures in Luke 24:32.

An expositor's role

The expositor should be able to take the Word of God
and to open men's eyes to the application of that Word

to everyday life. He is a servant of that Word and of the people. He is not there to impress the people with his fund of good stories or his cleverness in declaring his own views. He is to find what God has said and is still saying through the Scriptures and to apply that in the power of the Spirit to the hearts of the people and to his own heart.

Exposition may sound quite simple from the above description, but the sad fact is that few preachers engage in it. Our messages then carry little of the authority of God and His Word behind them, and while they may move our people temporarily, do not build them up in their faith or send them back to their Bibles to find out if these things are really so. Again, we may test ourselves by asking how many of our listeners even bring their Bibles with them, and when they do, how often they feel compelled to refer to them.

Study questions

Study Peter's sermon on the day of Pentecost — Acts 2: 14-42.
1. What passage of Scripture did Peter use as a basis?
2. How was this explained in terms of the needs and circumstances of his hearers?
3. What evidence do you find that Peter made men think? Trace the development of his argument. What was the climax?
4. How do you know Peter moved the *hearts* of the people? What particular words of his sermon were especially aimed to do this?
5. What did Peter expect the people to *do* as a result of his message?
6. How many deep theological ideas did Peter bring into his sermon? How were they relevant?

3

Planned preaching

Aim at nothing and you are sure to hit it. To preach on a different subject each week with no overall Spirit-guided plan in mind is to develop a congregation who have little overall grasp of the faith. Christian truth is a consistent whole. We are told to have our loins girded with the truth. The Roman soldier's armour held together because of the belt around his loins, and the Christian's armour holds together by an overall grasp of the truth as a body of teaching. How can we expect our people to have such a grasp of truth if they listen to a different preacher each week? To give the pulpit ministry to a visitor may be a sign of humility in a pastor but asks for spiritual weakness in a congregation. How also can they have an overall grasp of the truth if every Sunday's sermon is quite unrelated to what went before and what comes after? Regrettably, some Christians' spiritual diet consists only of the sermons they hear on Sunday. What kind of food do we plan for them?

I am convinced that regular expository preaching carefully planned ahead is the best way to feed a congregation. Let me give several reasons why.

Reasons for planned expository preaching

1. By preaching to a plan, whether it be by going through a book

*or by covering certain subjects, the whole of God's plan can
be unfolded*

We are delivered from being bound to our own pet
themes. Next Sunday we have to go on with the letter
to the Romans, or whatever it is, and we preach on what
the next passage says, not on what we would like it to
say. Have you ever sat under a preacher who has a pet
theme? The theme may be the ABC of the gospel, a very
good theme, but even that wears thin when he finds it in
every single passage and preaches on little else. The congregation, too, get to know what is coming and their
minds turn off at the start.

2. Regular exposition enables us to deal with some important matters of Christian living in a natural way

The life of Joseph contains the temptation to sexual sin
with Potiphar's wife. He would be a bold pastor who
suddenly and with no apparent reason chose that
passage for a sermon. People would ask themselves what
or whom he was getting at, or whether he himself had
some strange kink in his make-up. But this kind of subject needs dealing with today. So many Christians never
receive teaching to prepare them for marriage or to
enable them to face a world without moral standards. A
series of messages on Joseph's life would make it quite
natural to speak on sexual temptation without anyone
asking why.

3. As the congregation begin to hear planned expository preaching, they start to think ahead

They want to know what is going to happen next. They
may even be interested enough to look up a passage
before they come. While they are listening in church
they will be encouraged to refer to the passage to under-

stand its meaning, and therefore they are more likely to
bring their Bibles along. They are beginning to need
them. Furthermore, careful, simple exposition may set
them studying for themselves, and a spiritual, ethical,
time bomb will have been planted in their lives that will
eventually explode with untold benefit to the church.

4. Ethics, both personal and social will begin to take their place in the regular teaching

Most evangelical preaching is doctrinal. Doctrine is
especially vital today, with so many theologies without
content drifting around. The epistles are full of doctrine,
but they are also full of ethics. How often are these
ethical standards brought before people today? When
did you last hear or preach a sermon on employer/
employee relationships, husband/wife, parent/child relationships? Dishonesty in business causes untold agony
for Christians today. Do they know what the Bible says
about this and how the early Christians worked it out in
their day?

5. The Old Testament will have its place in planned expository preaching

How often does that happen in your local church? Yet
how up-to-date is Amos with his thundering denuncia-
tion of social injustice and oppression! How contemporary are God's judgements on unjust societies in
Isaiah and Jeremiah! How relevant to the questions we
ask are those that Habakkuk asked God! The gospel is
not primarily a social programme. Yet the gospel does
have social implications and sometimes, because we do
not teach them, thinking, caring people dismiss the
church as irrelevant. Haggai and Zechariah faced the
problems of a developing society striving to get on its

feet after seventy years of chaos and neglect and with a people depressed and despondent. The whole counsel of God includes all these issues.

Factors to consider in planned expository preaching

1. We must be careful first of all to ensure an adequate balance in our preaching

All ethics would be as bad as none at all. Some preachers have been able to go straight through a book like the letter to the Romans expounding just a verse or part of a verse each week and still maintain interest. Few of us can do this. By all means let us teach through Romans, but most of us will need to cover more than one verse in a week and to break off from the series every now and then to deal with something quite different. Variety is essential in any diet.

2. Then we should aim to cover the foundation truths of the faith at least once a year

Whether our denomination agrees or disagrees with 'the church's year' we should regularly cover the doctrines of the birth, death, resurrection and ascension of the Lord and His gift of the Spirit. Without regular reminders, Jesus' second coming and similar truths gradually cease to affect our thinking and our living. Forward thinking through a year enables us to cover what is needed.

3. In preserving a balance in our preaching we need to be very firm with ourselves about our pet themes

Having sat under a ministry that came back again and again each week to the same point, and having heard and seen the reaction of the congregation, I know how easily we can deceive ourselves. A good wife, or a faithful deacon or elder whom we trust, can help keep a check on us here.

4. We must also reckon on the spiritual, emotional and intellectual needs of our congregation.

The Corinthians could take only 'milk', but the Romans were obviously able to digest much more solid meat. To feed meat to babies leads to indigestion. To feed milk to mature adults will make them look elsewhere for food. They do not find what they need when they come. Nor must we confuse the grasp of spiritual truth with intellectual brightness. Some very clever people need 'milk' in spiritual matters and some very simple people by the guidance of the Spirit can rejoice in strong 'meat'.

Suggested expository series

Let me suggest some series of expositions. You may for instance take a self-contained section of the Word of God. The Lord's Prayer is a good example. By taking each clause of that prayer in successive weeks you will cover the following truths:

The fatherhood of God;
the transcendence of God — that is, He is not to be identified with His creation but is over against it; ·
the holiness of God;
the rule of God;
the will and purpose of God;
the place of material provision as a proper subject for prayer yet not the first in importance;
the need for forgiveness from God and of our fellow men;
the dependence of the believer on God's protection.

You will also have covered subjects like:

the place of prayer in Christian living;

prayer as submission and worship, not just asking for things;

the relative importance of material and spiritual matters in a materialistic age.

When you have finished, your people should know more of the nature of God, the place of prayer, and the right use of material possessions, and should be in a much better position to understand what it means to live as man should live, as a creature before his Creator.

Suggested expository subjects

1. You may decide to preach through a book

Jonah, for example, shows the reluctant missionary, racially prejudiced and determined at all costs to avoid God's pursuing love. The four chapters divide his story very effectively and even though a congregation may have few reluctant missionaries, there are usually several people running away from God, refusing His love, grumbling at His dealings with them, or forgetting God's love for those of other nations and races. Jonah is right up-to-date.

2. You may take the life of a Bible character

The life of a Bible character provides living illustrations of God's dealings with men. Their environment was different and the amount of knowledge they had to go on was much less, but they feared and hoped, schemed and planned, loved and hated, cheated and even murdered just as man still does.

3. You may take a chapter of the Bible

This might be something like John 19 or Mark 14,

tracing the last days and hours of Christ.

4. You may take a theme such as prayer, or the signs of Jesus' coming, or the work of the Holy Spirit

Whatever you do needs regular realistic assessment, continued planning and careful thought as to how long each series should be. Some people may fear the limiting of the Spirit of God in all this. There is no real basis for this fear. The Spirit can guide you six months ahead as easily as six hours or six minutes. If He tells you to scrap the subject for the day you can do it. He normally works through the minds of men in an orderly fashion. Planning can be as prayerful as last minute preparation.

A word of caution

One constant practice of many churches causes me great concern with regard to an expository ministry of planned preaching and teaching. So many congregations or pastors insist on a different person preaching each week. Sometimes the pastors travel round to different churches in turn. The result is haphazard unrelated preaching, congregations with a very small idea of what the faith is all about and an unhealthy desire to hear another new voice continually. A pastor, it seems, is not without honour save in his own church. So long as this system prevails, the people of God will remain without that grasp of the truth which alone can enable them to stand against the assaults of the enemy in a turbulent twentieth century.

Study questions

1. Draw up headings for a series of sermons on John 19, the life of Jacob and 1 Thessalonians.

2. Write down when you last preached, (or heard someone else preach) on marriage (not a wedding), Christian business methods, prayer, the second coming of Christ, and the meaning of repentance. What passages would you expound to teach these truths?

3. If you had (or have) the freedom to decide on a series of messages in your church to last six Sundays and you wanted to meet the most important spiritual needs of your congregation, what would you preach on, which Bible passages would you use and under what headings would you announce your six subjects?

4

The preparation – basic outlines

Now we move on to the practical details of preparing to expound the Scriptures. I am conscious that what I say from now on is very much how God has led me. I have a temperament and a cultural background probably quite different from yours, but God mediates truth through personality, so I trust that some of the things He has taught me may be of use to you.

Value of self-discipline

If you have planned your preaching you will of course be relieved of that agonizing search for a text. What you will preach on this week has already been decided. All you need to do is to discipline yourself to work on the passage until it yields its precious truths. Did I say 'all you need'? This discipline is the hardest battle of sermon preparation. To illustrate the value of such discipline let me give a word of testimony.

As a young minister I was expected to preach one Sunday at a youth service to which young people from seven years and upwards would come. The reading given for that Sunday in our denominational plan of readings was Luke 14:25-33. How could I speak to such young children from such a passage about hating father or mother? Yet I had no peace to move from that text, either then at the beginning of the week, or later when, conscious of the unsuitability, I desperately wanted to change. In the congregation on the Sunday morning was a Christian nurse who had recently led to Christ a woman from a very tough background. Because of earlier drinking habits this woman still suffered from depression. The day before she had been depressed again because her mother accused her of not showing love. 'You never take me for a drink now,' she said, 'you do not love me.' In fact the woman loved her mother now for the first time in her life. She could not stand the continual unjust accusation and had decided to abandon her Christian profession and to return to her old ways with her mother. 'Come to church just once more,' said the nurse. Reluctantly she came. When the Bible reading was announced she turned to the nurse and said, 'If he doesn't preach on that, I am through.' God's Spirit used a discipline to speak to a specific need, and that person is now a Christian worker.

How to prepare an expository sermon

How then should you tackle the passage of Scripture before you?

1. Study the passage thoroughly and soak yourself in its contents

Commentaries at this stage stifle your thinking and cramp your mind to think just as the commentator does. This limits the Spirit of God. Once you have the passage in your mind you can meditate upon it on various occasions during the week, for instance, walking along the street or waiting at bus stops. I suggest not when crossing the road! Coming back for small periods again and again often produces more valuable thought than persevering through one long stretch. This means of course starting early in the period available. One very fine expositor would roughly outline a message just as soon as he was invited to give it, even if the time of delivery was some way ahead. He could then spend any spare moments turning the passage over in his mind. By long exposure to thought and meditation the passage becomes part of you and speaks to your heart. Then the Spirit of God can put in your heart the particular application to the circumstances of your hearers.

2. *Ask yourself, 'What is the main thrust of this word to today's people and what points must be emphasized to bring home that main thrust to men's hearts?'*

These points *must arise* from the text or passage, otherwise you are imposing your view, not expounding God's. If that is the case, then, however sound your teaching may be, it will not and cannot carry the authority of the Word of God with it.

3. *Make your points clear and relevant*

'The ontological argument for creation' may arise from a text, but it will turn off the keenest congregation as quickly as a power failure turns out a light. You must not just ask, 'What does this say?' but 'What does this say to these people?' Your points must be *clear*. The congregation should be able to tell you the substance of those points at the end of the message. The test of teaching is whether the pupil learned, not whether the teacher covered his material. Clarity communicates.

4. *Present your main points in a logical manner*

They should be related. This relation may not be the relation of points in a straight line. They may be the relation of parts of a picture. But they should be related. Here there are basic differences in various cultures and languages. Western thought usually moves in a straight line, building up to a climax. Eastern thought and certainly Chinese language builds blocks into a total picture. Each part of a Chinese character adds something to the total meaning of a word. One character therefore may convey a total picture made up of different parts that in English would require a sentence to describe. 安 means peace. What is peace? English language would require even a paragraph to elaborate. By portraying one woman under one roof, Chinese has conveyed at least one meaning of peace by using two idea blocks that flash a pictorial message immediately. Similarly, Western preaching builds in a straight line to a climax, but Chinese preaching often uses several pictures or idea-blocks that communicate a message. The point I would stress here, however, is that the main points of the message, whether presented in Eastern or Western style, should be *clearly related both to the text and to each other.*

5. Stress your main points

Furthermore, if the main points are memorable they are more likely to be remembered! Some preachers have used alliteration so much that people are tired of it. Others have forced on main points headings that do not really fit. On the other hand, some can use clear headings naturally without making them sound forced and people find them easy to remember. Psalm 19, for example, divides very easily into three clear parts and these could well be headed: 1. God speaks through the universe (verses 1-6); 2. God speaks through His Word (verses 7-10); 3. God speaks to the heart (verses 12-13). Verse 14 then provides a closing prayer in the light of God's speaking.

6. Be sure to obtain the main aim of your sermon from the expository text itself

This may seem to be back to front but if you leave the definition of the aim of the message until this stage you will not be tempted to force the passage to fit the aim. True exposition explains what God is actually saying, not what you think He should be saying. You are the servant of the Word of God, a message-carrier not a message-creator. This main aim of the message is for your guidance as a preacher, not for the guidance of the hearers. If you accomplish the aim it will be clear enough to the hearers, but because you do not have to express it in words to them, you can describe this aim more fully to yourself and in terms you might not use in talking to others. My aim in speaking on Psalm 19 would be expressed like this: 'To show the inadequacy of general revelation, the fulness of special revelation and the need for human response to all revelation.' I would not use theological terms like 'general' and 'special' revelation to my hearers, but they clarify my own thinking as I prepare. My message will be fitted to accomplish my aim. Some things will be left out because they are not relevant to the aim. Others will be emphasized, and all will be streamlined to call forth a response in the heart of the hearers to God's wonderful revelation of Himself.

How to develop the main points of your message

You know the broad outline, but much remains to be filled in. God speaks through the universe, but what do you need to say about that? Verses 1-4 of Psalm 19 speak of God revealing His glory and His work through the universe. This revelation is poured forth and is continuous, twenty-four hours a day, (v.2). It is a silent

witness and yet a spoken one, and it is a universal witness (vv. 3,4). Take the following steps to develop your
main points:

1. Ask yourself whether you need to emphasize all these truths to achieve your aim

You could make a whole message from these verses
alone and if you include all of them you might either
lose your sense of direction towards your aim or lose
your congregation half-way; probably both. Most of us
try to include too much in our communication. Our
hearers' ability to receive is far less than our enthusiasm
to give.

2. Write down your thoughts in line with your aim, then ruthlessly cut out what is not relevant

When you are developing your points and fitting the
flesh to the skeleton outline you will probably find as I
do that to write down your thoughts is necessary. For
many people, writing stimulates thinking.

3. Build up to a climax that emphasizes your aim and then be prepared for a quick end

Too often a good message is ruined by a wandering
finish. We shall consider the conclusion in a separate
chapter, but for the moment note the need to work
steadily up to a climax, reach it and stop. The course of
your sermon, if plotted on a graph, should look roughly
like the graph on page 30.

Very often the second point of the sermon will bear
more exposition than the first or last. If you spend too
long on the first point the hearers may begin to wonder
just when it will all end. In that case by the time the
second section is finished the hearers may have had

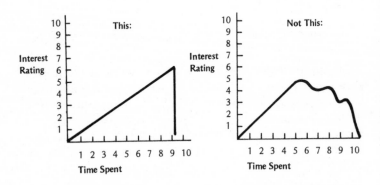

almost as much as they can take. But the middle section can stand longer time. In Psalm 19 this fits very well, for you would want to spend more time on revelation through God's Word than on the more general revelation conveyed by creation. Verses 7—10 of Psalm 19 tell us that God's Word revives and brings life to a dead soul, educates a man who wants to know, brings joy that truth has at last been found, opens the eyes to spiritual reality, never fails and tells us the right way to live. No wonder this Word is more valuable than the world's richest metal and sweeter than pure honey!

4. Decide how much or how little time you can give to each part and keep to that.

There will be times of course when the Holy Spirit will take charge and you will abandon everything that you have prepared. You must not be so bound to your outline that you cannot respond to such prompting. On the other hand, of course, the Spirit's overruling must not be made an excuse for no or poor preparation.

Once you have developed your theme to this extent you may realize that another Scripture is relevant to your exposition. Again the time available will decide how much you can include, as also will your hearers' knowledge of Scripture. You may only serve to confuse them by running about all over the Bible if they are not used to finding different books.

Study questions

1. Listen to someone preach. Try to decide what is his main aim and what are the main points of his message. How do they link together? If you can do this with a friend, check afterwards what in fact the main points and aim were.
2. Write out the main aim and main points for a sermon on the prodigal son, Luke 15: 11–32.
3. What was the main aim of Jesus' message to the disciples in John 14:12-31? Trace His thought as it moves from point to point. How did he fulfil His aim?
4. You are preparing a message on Psalm 19. Your second point is: 'God speaks through His Word.' Write out notes for what you would say under this heading, based on verses 7-10.

5

The exposition of narrative (or stories)

God's self-revelation to man

We have in the Bible God's revelation of Himself to men. This is what makes the Bible unique among religious books. The Bible is not a record of what men have thought about God, but of what God Himself has told us about Himself and ourselves. If I do not know a person I can learn something about him simply by looking at him, but how much I can learn that way, and how accurate my thinking will be, is another matter. In order really to get to know him I have to listen to him as he speaks to me and reveals himself to me. I learn what he is like by what he says and what he does. Person-to-person communication is quite inadequate without this self-revelation.

A progressive communication

God is personal; so are we. God deals with us in person-to-person communication. This progressive communication of God to man is found in the Scriptures and the methods God uses are the same as for other kinds of person-to-person communication — words and deeds.

God's revelation, especially in the early stages is as much by *act* as by *word*. Yet His Word is needed to interpret His acts. Some modern theologians will accept God's acts but cannot accept the Word that explains them. Yet very often we cannot understand what an act is all about unless it is accompanied by the word of explanation. So act and word go along together in the Bible. Sacrifices, for instance, would be senseless slaughter if God had not told us that 'without the shedding of blood there is no forgiveness of sins' (Heb. 9:22).

Psalm 103:7 records, 'He made known His ways unto Moses, His acts to the people of Israel.' Moses had close access to God and, whereas all the people could see what God did, Moses was privileged to learn why He did it and what He meant. God's works illustrate God's ways and His ways interpret His works.

This is one reason why Scripture is so fascinating. The Bible does not come as dead philosophy to tell us what we should be like, but portrays God at work in human lives just like ours, and shows how in the end He reveals Himself perfectly in one human life, that of the Son of God, the Word made flesh. The works of Scripture are displayed on the stage of human life and the words of Scripture are a God-given commentary on human life in relation to God. Revelation is not divorced from life and expressed in academic terms. Some of the words of Scripture arise from the deepest experiences of the human heart.

More than good stories

Because God has revealed Himself in acts and words, the narratives of the Bible are very important. They are much more than good stories of historical accounts. They contain within themselves a revelation by God Himself of His own character and of His will for men.

'Whatever was written in former days was written for our instruction, that by steadfastness and by the encouragement of the Scriptures we might have hope'

(Rom. 15:4). God guided the preparation of the Scriptures towards a particular end. He made sure by His Holy Spirit that what was recorded is effective and profitable for both steadfastness and encouragement, to enable Christians to remain firm under all circumstances and to strengthen their hope. The word for 'encouragement' comes from the same root as that used by Jesus to describe the Holy Spirit as the 'Comforter' in John 15:26; 16:7. God Himself is called the God of steadfastness and encouragement in the very next verse (Rom. 15:5), thereby underlining that the words of Scripture are not simply words of good advice but words which carry the power and authority of the living God and of His Holy Spirit.

Purpose of biblical narrative

Scripture, then, is a kind of divine casebook in which human circumstances, fears, hopes, failings and anxieties are expressed in living examples, and God's answers to human problems live before our eyes. Paul in writing to the Corinthians outlines the story of the exodus from Egypt and then declares that 'these things are warnings for us, not to desire evil as they did' and that 'these things happened to them as a warning' but they were written down for our instruction, upon whom the end of the ages has come' (1 Cor. 10:6,11). Scripture narrative is not meant to be just a good story, but an educational guide in the school of life. The stories of Scripture are therefore as vital to our instruction as the passages of doctrine. They clothe the truth in flesh and blood and make it easier for us to understand.

In accordance with this way of presenting truth, John describes Jesus' miracles not simply as wonders, but as 'signs' carrying a much deeper meaning than an isolated set of marvellous actions could possibly do. Modern television has learned from the biblical method. Some of the most popular programmes are series on the lives and actions of one family or set of characters. By embodying certain ideas in these characters, the broadcaster communicates to the receiver the emotions and reactions he wants that receiver to experience. The aim may be to make the viewer willing to have a smallpox vaccination or to make him adopt a certain political or social outlook. The world uses this method to communicate ideas but, even in countries where people still love stories and the art of story-telling is highly developed, it is sad that there is so very little preaching on the story passages of the Old Testament. Indeed to many the Old Testament is a closed book. Yet a church that is not taught in the Old Testament usually has a weak idea of the greatness, majesty and holiness of God and is liable to be shallow in its approach to evangelism. We neglect Bible stories at our peril.

Using biblical narratives for expository preaching

How then do you deal with a story for preaching purposes? One of the very first things you do is to:
1. Think yourself into the circumstances of the story;
2. Use your imagination;
3. Live out the drama in your own mind;
4. Imagine how each of the characters must have been feeling at different times;
5. Ask yourself why the characters acted or reacted as they did and what they felt like as they did it.

A story that has never lived for you will never live for your hearers. One of the most memorable sermons I have heard was on the healing of the paralysed man let down through the roof. The preacher saw the miracle of healing through the eyes of four different people, pictured in his imagination as the four men who carried the sick man. What they felt was derived from the truths of the passage, but the result of using this method was that all of us could identify in our thoughts and emotions with these different men. Remember that although our outward living conditions may be different from those of biblical days, men still have the same desires, fears, hopes, ambitions and sorrows. The human condition never changes, nor does God.

Test your story-telling talent

A good exercise in testing yourself on your ability to make stories live is to tell them or read them to children. Children love stories and react spontaneously with interest or boredom, so they give a more honest response. Training yourself to be responsive and sensitive to children's reactions is a wonderful preparation and discipline for a preacher.

Probing questions

Having soaked yourself in the atmosphere of a story until you can see the glint of the sun on Goliath's spear, or touch the hem of Jesus' robe in the crowd, begin to ask yourself these questions:
1. Who are the main people involved?
2. What can I discover about the attitudes, motives, thoughts and reactions of each person?
3. What is the main aim of the story in this context?
4. What is the context in which this story appears in the Scripture?

An example of the importance of the context comes in Matthew 22:41-46. Jesus asked a question of the Pharisees about the Christ being the Son of David. This story cannot be rightly understood except in the light of the searching questions the lawyers and Sadducees had been asking Christ. Seen in that context, Jesus' question brilliantly stopped all argument, silenced the opposition and boldly claimed His own divinity. His enemies had no answer and their enforced silence said more than hours of teaching could possibly have done.

How to prepare a biblical narrative for exposition

Let me now illustrate the method of dealing with narrative from Mark 12:41-44. In the early days of using this (and often when more used to preparing messages, too) I have found it helpful to write down the words of the passage and, in doing so, to highlight the main verbs, the action words of the story, indenting the various phrases more or less, depending on how important they are to the whole.

The story of the poor widow and her mite then looks something like this:

1. The context

Jesus disputed with the Pharisees and condemned them for making too much of religious actions and too little of heart motives.

2. The main people involved

Jesus, the rich people, the poor widow.

3. What can be learnt from each person?

(Here is where I collect together what is said about each person as below. The right-hand column comes in useful later on.)

1. Jesus
v.41   He sat down

```
        watched
v.43    spoke, Truly, I say to
            you,
            This poor widow
            has put in more
            more than all those who
            are contributing.
        They all contributed
        out of abundance
        she out of poverty
            everything she
                had
            her whole living.
```

2. The rich

```
v.41    Many of them
        put in large sums.
```

3. The widow

```
v.42    Poor
        put in two copper coins
v.44    out of her poverty
        put in all that she had
```

Now you are in a position to use the right-hand
column. I have found it very helpful to note down in
that column anything that strikes me about the words
and the truth in the first column. For instance, Jesus'
sitting down and watching spoke to me of a deliberate
action on His part to call attention to the importance of
the lesson being lived out before the disciples' eyes.
Again, His use of the phrase, 'Truly, I say to you,' told
me He was making an important statement. If you go
through the story in this way many fresh thoughts will
strike you. They must of course come out from what is
said and not be pure invention, but if you meditate on
the words many thoughts will come to you, and if you
write them down they will not be lost. They can be put

together in clear order later. Some of them you may never use in your message; others you may use on another occasion.

1. Jesus

v.41	He sat down	deliberate action
	watched	God sees and cares
v.43	spoke, Truly, I say to you	important statement
	This poor widow	individual counts
	has put in more	God's method of
	more than all those who are contributing	arithmetic
	They all contributed	what is *left* after
	out of abundance	giving is important
	she *out of poverty*	
	everything she had	all is God's
	her *whole living*	wholehearted giving

2. The rich

v.41	Many of them	majority not always right
	put in large sums.	seen of men

3. The widow

v.42	Poor	not what we have that counts
	put in two copper coins	not worthless because of the person
v.44	out of her poverty	God sees. (Unaware of being watched)
	put in all that she had	minimum subscription is all we have
		riches can hinder us doing this.

Now you are in the position to answer the question, 'What is the main aim of the story?' You have to think this through carefully. I discovered two possible main aims for this story. They should be thought of as alternatives rather than trying to use both of them at the same time. One of the aims could be to illustrate how God looks on the heart and not on the appearance. The other could be to show that when we give to God it is not what we have given, but what we have left that counts. You would decide which aim to pursue and use your material accordingly. Perhaps I should make it quite clear at this point that I am using the word 'story' in the sense of a true description of events that actually took place, not in the sense of a story thought up to illustrate truth. Biblical stories are some of the most wonderful in the world, and all the more so because they are not human inventions, but true.

The following is a possible outline for a sermon with the first of these aims in mind. It is not developed but set out in a bare outline that would obviously need much work done on it, and it would also need introducing and finishing off.

Three things to notice about this incident in the Gospel of Mark:

1. God watches and He cares

Jesus deliberately sat down there.
He carefully watched what went into the treasury.
Probably few people noticed Him there and less thought of His opinion.
So God is concerned and watching over each of us.
Notice that Jesus was not picking fault, but noticing the generosity of the widow.
She was not too poor, too weak, or too old to matter.

2. The judgement men made

There were many rich people.
Everyone was thinking how much they were giving.
Some probably made a loud noise in throwing their

coins through the brass opening in the chest.
They did genuinely put in large sums.
They were no doubt well-dressed and respectable.
Most people probably did not see the widow come silently and drop in her tiny piece.

3. The judgement of God

He noticed the individual
He assessed her gift as the most valuable
  because they gave *out of riches*
  she gave *out of poverty*
  because she gave everything, all that she had.
God's judgement reversed the judgement of men.

Conclusion to be drawn

God looks more on inward motive than on outward action.
God's judgement is always accurate because He can look on the heart.
We should be very careful in making judgements. We need not fear because we are only one, or poor, or weak or old.
God sees and knows and cares.

The parts of this message can be expanded but, of course, you must be careful about how much time you give to each. Do not spend so much time on the first parts that you do not have enough time left to reach the main point that you intend to pass on.

Almost any narrative can be dealt with using this approach, whether from the Old or New Testament. By writing down your thoughts and meditations, you make them clear and firm. Writing them down also often leads to new thoughts' coming to mind. Narratives are the easiest passages to bring alive to a congregation. People

are interested in people and can identify with them, so
we should make maximum use of the stories of people
that God has provided for us in the Scriptures.

Study questions

1. Write out Mark 10:46-52 as suggested in this chapter.
   Then fill in the right-hand column and from this
   pick out what would be your main headings for a
   message.
2. Read a passage from a classical or modern story
   book to a friend or into a tape recorder. Ask your
   friend to comment on, or ask yourself the following:
       Does this story live, the way I read it?
       Does the tone of my voice vary or is it
           monotonous?
       How could I make this sound more interesting?
3. Tell the story of Zacchaeus, Luke 19:1-10, as
   though it happened last week in your town, using
   modern equivalents.
4. Describe exactly how Peter and John individually
   felt when they went into the tomb and discovered
   that Jesus' body was not there.

6

Exposition of the Psalms

One of the saddest lacks in the church today is our failure to make adequate use of the psalms. When did you last hear an exposition of the psalms and when did you last speak from a psalm? I think you will find that it is quite hard to remember when. Yet the psalms are a treasury of devotion and worship, and of human experience without parallel anywhere in the world.

The psalms have been described as the hymn book of Israel, for they were written to be sung. Like all good hymns they express particular experiences in general terms, so that, although we may not be facing the particular experience, we can share in the feelings of the psalmist and identify with him. Perhaps I can illustrate what I mean from the hymn which begins, 'O love that will not let me go.' This hymn arose out of the particular experience of George Matheson. He was engaged to be married, but then began to go blind. His fiancée decided that she could not go through with the marriage, and he was left terribly disappointed. He found consolation in the love of the Lord who would not let him go, and in renewed dedication of himself to that Lord. Many people who sing that hymn today know nothing of George Matheson's own experience. Many, however, have been able to identify with him because they have been facing other disappointments, such as failure to get a certain job, the failure of a close friend they are rely-

ing on for help, and so on. A good hymn will always
have the power to speak from a particular problem to
many other problems.

In the psalms, there is scarcely any human emotion or
experience that is not expressed. The deep penitence of
Psalm 51 is matched by the joyous praise of Psalm 150.
Psalm 73 portrays the perplexity of the righteous when
the wicked seems to be prospering and the righteous to
be suffering. Sorrow, bitterness, comfort, fear, despair,
hope, trust in darkness, vindication and praise are all expressed in different ways. The Book of Psalms offers a
rich mine of valuable material for the preacher to work
on. The Lord Jesus often quoted the psalms. These are
quoted in many places in the New Testament.

A poetic form

In tackling the psalms we must recognize that they are
hymns and they are poetry. Hence, we must understand
something about Hebrew poetry. Every country has its
own poetic forms, not readily understood by people
from a different culture. Hebrew poetry is no exception.
Western poetry until quite recently was based on rhyme
and rhythm. Hebrew poetry never was. Parallelism is the
basis of Hebrew poetry. The way it works is that an idea
is expressed in a certain way in one line. Then the idea
may be repeated in the next line in different words, or
contrasted with another opposite idea, or developed
further in another direction, or followed through to
completion. The second line again may be related to the
first as effect is related to cause. Let me illustrate: 'Pro-
long the life of the king,' is the first line of Psalm 61:6
and the second line repeats the thought by adding, 'May
his years endure to all generations.' The basic thought is
the same, but it is expressed in different words. Psalm

110:5 develops the thought of the first line in the second one: 'The Lord is at your right hand; he will shatter kings on the day of his wrath.' In the same psalm the second line of verse 7 is the effect that flows from the first line: 'He will drink from the brook by the way; therefore he will lift up his head.' Understanding how Hebrew poetry works provides help in understanding the message of a psalm.

Guidelines in expounding psalms

1. Find out as much as possible about the experience that lies behind the psalm

If you know what the psalmist was facing, then you have a much clearer idea of the full meaning of his words. Psalm 51 becomes much more meaningful when you realize that this is David's confession of sin after his adultery with Bathsheba and his murder of Uriah the Hittite. This psalm is without parallel in showing what true repentance and confession really mean. You do not have to limit its application to sexual sins, because repentance is basically the same for any sin and everyone needs true repentance if he is ever to prosper in the Christian life. Psalm 3 is clearly the expression of a man surrounded by enemies and tempted to despair and fear. The heading of the psalm suggests that at this particular time David was fleeing the kingdom after the rebellion of his son Absalom. Knowing that makes the feelings he expressed even more moving, but you can apply the message of the psalm to any modern situation where troubles abound and seem insurmountable, and where it is hard to sleep at night for worrying about them. Not all of the psalms can be traced to particular incidents. Many of them are the experiences of Israel as a nation and can be applied to groups rather than individuals, but where a historical background is brought to our attention or is pretty clear from the wording of the psalm, we have the possibility of deep enrichment.

2. Discover where possible the separate stanzas that go to make up the psalm.

Again, this is not always possible because some of the psalms do not appear to have been written in this way, but where the stanzas can be identified you have a great help to clearer exegesis. Some Bibles are printed with the psalms so divided up. Of course, the Hebrew stanzas do not in any way coincide with the division into verses in our Bibles, but are rather several verses put together. Psalm 1 clearly divides into two stanzas, the one drawing a picture of the godly righteous man and the other a picture of the ungodly. The two stanzas stand in direct contrast to each other and in this case give a very clear distinction to be used in constructing the points of your sermon.

3. Study the problem that faced the psalmist, and find out all you can about how he tackled the problem

How for example did he find help in God? What did he ask for? What truths about God Himself did he find helpful to him? What was the end result of the action he took? In Psalm 3 the problem faced by David was that of a great many enemies who were rising up against him, and most of whom had written him off as being beyond the help even of God. He tackled the problem in his own heart by thinking upon God as his shield, his glory and his vindicator. He turned all this into prayer in confidence that God would answer and the practical results were a good night of sleep (which, no doubt, he needed) and an ability to face an overwhelming enemy without the paralysing effect of fear. In fact, we know that eventually he was restored to his kingdom. The important point for a message, however, is the practical effect of meditating on the power of God to keep us, and the power of prayer to settle our minds, however great our problems in life. Prayer in this context is the secret to a good night's sleep in the midst of worry, to a heart at peace in the midst of violent opposition.

4. Relate the particular problem of the psalmist to the present problems of your own congregation

None of them are kings who have been put off their thrones by a *coup d'état*, but quite a number of them are surrounded by so many difficulties that they probably feel that even God cannot help them out of them. Some of the people may not be sleeping too well, and a message on this psalm could make all the difference to them as the Holy Spirit applies the Word to their hearts.

At times you will realize that the psalmist himself has not found his way through to the answer. The psalm may leave many questions unanswered, but this in itself is so true to life. The Lord never promised that we would always have quick easy answers to our problems or that we would never have outstanding questions to which we do not have an answer. To be honest and share with your congregation that this is not only true, but is the universal experience of the people of God down the ages, can encourage them to know that their experience is not unique.

Practical application

Once again, I have often found it helpful to write out

the psalm, keeping the right-hand column free for noting what I have learnt from the text and only using that column after completing the left-hand one. As an exercise you might like to cover the right-hand column below with a piece of blank paper and write down what you learn alongside the writing in the left-hand column, before comparing your thinking with mine. I have taken Psalm 95 because this is a psalm about worship that is very relevant to our subject.

Analysis of Psalm 95

v.1 O come let us sing to the Lord	singing worship
let us make a joyful noise to the rock of our salvation	joyful noise worship
v.2 let us come into His presence with thanksgiving	thanksgiving worship; worship is coming into His presence
let us make a joyful noise to Him with songs of praise	songs of praise
v.3 *For* the Lord is a great God a great king above all gods	*reason for praise* is God is great and supreme
v.4 In His hand are the depths of the earth	God controls creation in the deep
the heights of the mountains also	
v.5 the sea is His	in the height in the sea
He made it	God made the world
His hands formed the dry land	God made the land
v.6 O come, let us worship and bow down,	giving worth to God humbling ourselves
let us kneel before the Lord our Maker	position of humility before our Creator
v.7 For He is *our* God	but also *our* God in a special way
we are the people of His pasture, the sheep of His hand	we are related to Him as sheep to a shepherd here is prayer and adora-

		tion of God
	O that today you would hearken to His voice	God speaks to His people
v.8	harden not your hearts	the sermon in worship listening or hardening
	as at Meribah as on the day at Massah in the wilderness	lesson from Ex. 17:1-7
v.9	when your fathers tested me and put me to the proof	refusal to listen and obey was testing of God
v.10	for forty years I loathed that generation	God's reaction
	and said, 'They are a people that do err in heart	refusal to His Word is to err
	they do not regard my ways'	to refuse His ways
v.11	*therefore* I swore in my anger that they should not enter into my rest.	provokes God's wrath deprives of blessing.

An interpretation

As I looked again over what I had written down I realized that the psalm falls naturally into three stanzas, one of which begins in the middle of one of our verse divisions. The *first* section from verses 1-5 is an invitation to worship God in praise, joy, even a joyful noise, singing and thanksgiving, simply because He is God who made the world and keeps it going. This is a general invitation to all to worship their Creator and such worship is meant to be a joyful occasion. The *second section* is in a quieter key, calling for humble adoration and bent knees. The invitation here is more personal and limited to those who can say that the Lord is their God, they are His people and He is their Shepherd. Only the true believer who knows the great Shepherd of the sheep can possibly join in this kind of worship. Verses 6-7b cover this section. *The rest of the psalm* is very solemn indeed and has reference to hearing

God speak to the congregation, warning them that they should listen carefully and not in any way harden their hearts. The stern lesson of Israel in the wilderness is put before them. Their obedience and response to the Word of God now determines their future enjoyment of God's blessings. I found in this psalm a pattern for worship, including singing, thanksgiving and praise, prayer, adoration and quiet worship, and then finally the ministry of the Word of God. It is interesting to note here, too, that listening to the Word of God is not an added extra to the rest of the service, nor does it take up nearly all the time, but it is an important part in a balanced diet of worship, whereby God may speak to us as well as our speaking to Him. Maintaining this balance is never easy. Some churches confine the preacher to ten minutes, as though the sermon were a tolerated nuisance, while others expect the preacher to begin after a hymn and prayer hastily disposed of, as though God were not worthy of our best offering of praise and adoration.

The important point, however, is that the setting out of a psalm like this can help you to see what the structure of it is and what lessons you can gain from it. You will notice the way I have deliberately listed the 'let us' phrases one under the other. This helps towards clear comparison. You will notice too that I have put the words 'for' and 'therefore' in italics. That is because these are important link words in Scripture giving us reasons why certain things follow each other. The reference to Exodus 17 of course opens another whole sphere for illustrating the dangers of disobeying the Word of God. You have to decide how much or how little of the detail of that illustration you want to, or have time to, use. Again, you will almost certainly have far too much material for one sermon in the psalm and you have the difficult task of deciding what to leave out in order to express the main theme of the psalm or the part of it on which you will preach.

The psalms touch the devotional heart of the Word of God. If you can introduce your people to these songs and give them a taste of what it means to identify with the joys and sufferings, hopes and fears of the people who wrote them, you will have done a deep service to the people of God in our day.

Study questions

1. Analyse Psalm 67 according to the suggested pattern and outline a message on the psalm.
2. What kind of circumstances do you think caused Psalms 53, 70, 72 and 115 to be written?
3. In Psalm 121 what are modern equivalents in our experience of 'the hills' of verse 1, the 'shade' of verse 5, the thoughts expressed in verse 6, and the 'going out and coming in' of verse 8?
4. How would you plan to preach on Psalm 119?

7

Expounding the Epistles

A challenging expository subject

The letters of the New Testament present the most rewarding and yet challenging parts of the Scriptures for
the expositor. The problem is not so much what to say
as what to leave out, and how to do justice to a passage
packed with rich material. The mind of a man like Paul
was so filled with ideas, and the object of his thinking
was so glorious and abounding that as Peter himself con-
fessed in a major understatement, 'There are some
things in them (i.e. Paul's Epistles) hard to understand.'
Our job is not only to understand as much as we can,
but also to communicate to our brethren in terms that
they can understand and that are relevant to their daily
lives. These letters are often closely argued documents.
They are full of detailed truth and careful shades of
meaning. In them every single word is full of signifi-
cance. Expounding them therefore calls for hard work
by the preacher before he can ever begin to put a
message together.

I have found the following principles very helpful in
using the Epistles.

Guidelines in expounding the Epistles

1. Take note of the main verbs and the tenses used in these verbs

They are the action words and they govern the whole of

the rest of the sentence. In this connection a knowledge of the original Greek is tremendously helpful. Greek was a much more accurate language than English and capable of very delicate shades of meaning. If you have not been able to study Greek for yourself, check up if you can with the aid of suitable commentaries that will explain the important differences. Even if you cannot do that because you do not have commentaries available, do not give up on the Epistles. There is still a wealth of spiritual truth available to you, but be sure to take notice of the verbs that are used. An example of the importance of verbal forms is in Ephesians 5:18: 'Be filled with the Spirit.' The command is not to have a once-for-all experience, but to be under the constant control of the Holy Spirit. As it is given as a command it is something for which we are responsible and not something that we have to wait for God to do for us.

2. Notice the positives and negatives that come in the passage

Scripture does not always define things positively. Sometimes we are told what is not right, or what something is not, rather than what it is, and this helps us in our understanding. Do not be afraid of the negatives. 1 Corinthians 13 is an example of this. Verses 4 to 6 read: 'Love is patient and kind' — a very positive statement, but then it goes on: 'Love is *not* jealous or boastful, it is *not* arrogant or rude. Love does *not* insist on its own way; it is *not* irritable or resentful; it does *not* rejoice at wrong, but rejoices in the right.' An emphasis on the negative helps us to highlight the positive, just as a good 'negative' in photography is necessary for a sharp final print. The Epistles often place the negative and positive alongside each other and we should take full account of this.

Another important feature of the Epistles is the use

of prepositions like 'in', 'by', 'with', 'to', 'through'.
Greek used many prepositions, in order to give fine
shades of meaning. Some modern languages use many of
them, but others use very few, and if your own language
is one of the latter, then you may need to give greater
thought as to how to convey the meaning of the Epistles
to your hearers. You may also be tempted to overlook
the importance˙ of some of these words. Conjunctions
are also very important for they connect one line of
argument with another. 'And', 'but', 'therefore',
'because' can carry important meanings for the
expositor.

3. Have the main theme of the passage clear in your mind before you begin to interpret the details

Otherwise you can misinterpret what the Scripture is
really saying. This is particularly true when you are
speaking on passages about which Christians are not
completely agreed, such as those relating to doubtful
things, or to spiritual gifts. A grasp of the main argument and an understanding of the problem with which
the apostle was dealing will keep you from unbalanced
presentations. Attention to the main verbs will help you
again here, for they hold the whole passage together.

4. Know the circumstances of the people to whom the letter was written wherever that is possible

To know something of the Gnostic heresy that John was
facing when he wrote his letters helps you to understand
some of his wording. To know that Paul was tackling a
situation where people were going back to salvation by
works and law-keeping in Galatians helps you to understand why he wrote so strongly and why what he says
may seem to contradict some of James's writing. In fact

James was tackling the reverse situation where people were relying on a head knowledge that produced no practical result in their lives.

5. Decide early on how you will approach the Epistle

If you have unlimited time before you, you may want to preach through the Epistle. But then this may take a matter of years, if you preach once a week and expound the details of the book. Most of us have neither the ability to sustain such a long series nor the congregation that will be content to listen, so you have to decide what main themes you will develop, or what parts you will leave out, or where you will stop and take some other subject. Consecutive preaching builds up the faith of the people, but there is no point in losing their interest by continuing with the same series too long. One of the hardest tasks of the preacher is choosing what treasures to leave out.

6. Keep a careful check on the subjects you choose, to ensure an adequate balance of teaching

One thing to beware of in taking the Epistle is lest you always preach on the doctrinal part or always preach on the ethical part. Most of the Epistles begin with doctrine and then lead on to the ethical results of such doctrines. To preach on the ethics without the doctrine is to leave ethics without any base, and to preach on doctrine without ethics is to leave doctrine in the air and unrelated to life on the shop-floor or in the market. All of us have our own pet themes and part of the aim of exposition is to keep us from going back to them all the time.

7. Follow the rules of biblical interpretation

Such rules as not interpreting one passage of Scripture

in a way that contradicts the plain teaching of another part are vital. A full list of such principles of interpretation is beyond the scope of this book. One thing, however, I would like to say. I find that many lay people come to the Bible with a conscious or unconscious feeling that because it is God's Word inspired by His Spirit, somehow the ordinary rules of language do not apply. If, therefore, I ask them what a particular verse says on some subject they will often ignore the plain meaning of the words and come out with some safe phrase that they remember about the gospel, such as, 'We must all believe in Jesus.' The verse may say nothing of the kind, but there seems to be an in-built feeling that the plain words cannot possibly mean what they actually say, and there must be some deeper meaning known only to those who have studied for the ministry. Preachers have sometimes been responsible for this sad fact, because they have drawn somewhat fanciful pictures from passages that were never meant to say such things. Because the congregation cannot see the connection between the passage and the picture, they assume that there must be something wrong with the way they look at the Bible, instead of something being very wrong with the preacher. Our job, however, is not to make the plain meaning look difficult, but to make plainer that which is already plain, and to send the congregation home feeling that they want to look at that passage again, because it has become so clear to them.

Practical application

Once again, in expounding the Epistles, I have found it helpful to write out a passage with two columns. This time, because there is so much to be learnt from the letters I have put fewer words on each line. You might

like to cover the right-hand column below with a blank
piece of paper and see if you can receive help by jotting
down your own conclusions.

Analysis of Ephesians 1

Dealing with Epistles

v.3 Blessed be the God of our
        Lord Jesus Christ
        and Father
    who has blessed us
        in Christ

        with every spiritual
        blessing
    in the heavenly places

1. *God has blessed*
    in Christ — sphere of
      blessing
    scope — all inclusive
    type — spiritual
    area — in spiritual realm

v.4 *even as He* chose us
        in Him

1. *God has chosen*
    in Christ — sphere of
      choice
    eternal love

        before the foundation of
        the world
        that we should be holy
            and blameless
            before Him

a. *Purpose* not pride
    but holiness and purity
    not before man but before
    God.

v.5 He destined us
        in love

1. *God has destined*
    in love — sphere of destiny
    source of confidence

        to be His sons
        through Jesus Christ
        according to the pur-
        pose of His will

a. *Purpose* — sonship
    means — through Jesus
    source — God's plan

v.6 to the praise of His
        glorious grace
        which He freely
        bestowed on us
        in the Beloved

effect — praise to Him

b. Cost to man — nil
    free gift
    in Christ

v.7 in Him we have redemption

why through Jesus? Need

through His blood
the forgiveness of our
trespasses
v.8 according to the riches
of His grace
which He lavished on us

for redemption — price
c. Cost to Christ — death
forgiveness — what is
obtained
motive — grace
abundance — lavished on
us

v.9 *For He* has made known
to us
in all wisdom
and insight
the mystery of His will
according to His purpose
which He sent forth in Christ
v.10 as a plan for the fulness of
time
to unite all things

1. *God has made known*
revelation —
kind and manner

the secret exposed
source — His plan
sphere — in Christ
timing —

a. Purpose — Gathering up
all into Christ

in Him
things in heaven and
on earth

sphere
extent

An interpretation

Let me now comment on this analysis. You will notice first of all that by starting in from the margin it is comparatively easy to see the *main verbs*. You see here that God has blessed us, (v.3), chosen us, (v.4), destined us, (v.5), and made known to us, (v.9). As I discovered this, on going down the right-hand column, I could see that an outline for a sermon comes right away. The theme would be: 'The great things God has done for us.' The main sections could be developed in terms of God's choice before the foundation of the world, leading to our being holy and blameless before Him; God's destining us, leading to our being sons of God; God's making known to us, leading to our sharing in what He is doing; and God's blessing us with every spiritual blessing leading us to have all that we need to fulfil our destiny. Obviously there would be enough, and more than enough, to keep us going for some time.

Then you will notice the *prepositions*. We are blessed *in* Christ, and *in* heavenly places. We are destined *in* love *through* Jesus Christ *according to* the purpose of His will. We have redemption *through* His blood *according to* the riches of His grace. Just by taking one of these prepositions and the fact that the Christians here were Ephesians, you can indicate for instance that a Christian lives in three places at once. He lives in Ephesus or some other place in the world. He lives in Christ, where God has provided everything for him. He also lives in heavenly places, where Christ is, but also where there are evil powers warring against him.

I have already indicated the main points of a possible message based on the main verbs. Again, as I went down the right-hand column a second time, I realized that on at least three occasions the purpose of God's action is mentioned. Predestination, on the basis of these verses, is not meant to make a person proud but to lead to holiness and blamelessness, and the aim is also that we should be the sons of God. The ultimate purpose is to sum up all things in Christ. A sermon could then be prepared on the purpose of God for His people, in terms of their moral living and the call to holiness, on their enjoyment of their position as sons of God, and on their part in the overall purpose of God for His whole creation in summing up all things in Christ.

By moving down the column again a third time, I discovered a contrast between the cost to man of this wonderful salvation and the cost to Christ. For us there is the glorious grace freely bestowed upon us in the Beloved. For Him there is the price of His blood so

freely shed for us. This is not a main theme of the
passage, and I would not take this particular contrast as
the basis for a sermon, but it might be very helpful to
draw attention to the contrast in the process of developing one of the main themes of the passage. You will
notice that I have used different numberings and letter-
ing in the right-hand column to distinguish different
themes. This numbering and the italics I put in after
having completed the notes in the right-hand column.
The following might be the outline of a sermon based
on the main verbs in this passage.

Subject: The wonderful things God has done for His people

1. He chose us

Notice this was done in Christ — there is no salvation
without Him   v.4
    before the foundaton of the world — if
    God chose us then He will not let us go.   v.4

2. He destined us

Notice this was an act done *in love*   v.5
    the purpose of this destiny is that we should
    be His sons — there is a present purpose in God's
    so acting;   v.5
    we become His sons through Jesus Christ;   v.5
    and this is possible because in Him we have
    redemption through His blood;   v.7

3. He made known to us the mystery of His will

God has revealed His love to us and not left us in the
dark.   v.9
His plan is to unite all things in Christ — by being in

Christ now
we are part of that divine plan for the whole
universe.   v.10
What a privilege is ours!

4. He has blessed us with every spiritual blessing

God has given us everything we need.
All of it is found in Christ.
All of it has already been given.

Application

If God has already done so much for us, we ought to be
the most joyful people alive.
If God has done all this, we need never fear He will let
us go.
If God has done all this, we ought to be living holy lives
that glorify Him.

This is of course the barest of outlines and, as I wrote
it, I was conscious of the vast amount of material con-
tained in it. Very careful selection would need to be
made of the points to be expanded. You will notice also
that no introduction is mentioned, because that is dealt
with elsewhere. The point I want to make, however, is
that these great truths are there in the Scriptures and
they only need drawing out and putting before us in
order to come to life, and that is our job as preachers of
the Word.

Study questions

1. Prepare an outline of a message on justification by
   faith from Romans 5:1-11.
2. What were the circumstances behind John's Second
   and Third Epistles, as far as you can tell from the
   letters themselves, without the help of commen-

taries?

3. List the main verbs of 1 Timothy 4:6-16. What do
   you need to do in the light of these verbs to make
   yourself a more effective preacher? Express this in
   terms of practical decision to be acted upon.
4. How would you plan a series of messages on a long
   book like Romans?

8

Expounding the Prophets

A difficult but rewarding expository subject

If the Epistles present the most rewarding and challenging section of the Scriptures for the expositor, the prophets represent the most difficult part. They spoke to a situation that was so different from ours, as far as outward circumstances are concerned, and used such different language forms from our everyday speech that we find them very hard to follow. But we are told that all Scripture is inspired by God and is profitable, and when we get behind the prophets and into them we find some of the most up-to-date messages from God to us. We must remember that a prophet was not primarily someone who foretold what was going to happen, but someone who told forth what God thought about what was actually happening when he spoke. The prophets are God's commentary on the religious, social, moral and political life of the time. Inasmuch as man is still the same in himself and still faces problems in ordering his society, the prophets still provide a commentary that is relevant today. Sometimes people complain that Christians have nothing to say about the problems of society. That was never true with the prophets, and if we faithfully expound them we shall have something to say, too. In Amos 8:5 he complains against the materialistic businessman who could not wait for the religious festival to be over so that he could get back to buying and selling, and who made the ephah, with which he measured the grain, smaller than it should have been, and the shekel, with which he weighed the customers' money, bigger than it should have been. Dishonest business did not die out with Amos; only the methods have changed. If we were expounding Amos 8 we should be morally bound to preach on this subject.

Guidelines in expounding the prophets

1. Find out all you can about the circumstances of the day, the way people lived, their fears and problems, their good and bad points

Then you can understand better the kind of message the prophet was bringing them from God. Many of the prophets lived in days of chaos and crisis very similar to our own, when governments were changing and society seemed to be falling apart and when the life of the ordinary people was very hard. Unfortunately the only way to find out about these circumstances is to read commentaries that explain them to us. While you can learn a certain amount from such passages as that quoted in Amos above, you can never get the full background of the prophets from their own writings. Even the reading of a good book on the history of Israel will help you to understand, for instance, why Jeremiah takes such a sad line, and why Haggai talks about earning wages 'to put them into a bag with holes', a most fitting illustration of the problems of inflation.

2. Discover as far as possible the human experiences of the prophet and his people

Men do not really change over the years and you are preaching to a human condition. You therefore want to know just what the condition was then and to translate that experience into that of your hearers. To take Haggai again, the first few verses make it clear that some people had managed to build fairly luxurious houses since they had returned from exile in Babylon, because they had panelled walls. Yet at the same time they had 'sown much and harvested little; you eat, but you never have enough; you drink, but you never have your fill; you clothe yourselves, but no one is warm'. Obviously the economy was not doing very well. This was the human condition that the prophet found, and it is one that is very common in many countries today.

3. Know what God had to say to this human condition, and the answers He was giving to the people

Haggai was told by God that the reason their harvests were not very good was because the Lord deliberately frustrated their hopes and when they had gathered in their little harvest He 'blew it away'. In other words this was an act of judgement on God's part. The reason for this act of judgement was that the people had completely neglected the building of the house of God. They had panelled houses for themselves, but God's house 'lies in ruins'. They had their priorities wrong. They were professing believers but were living as materialists, refusing to put God first. You do not need to look very far to see a clear application to many of our circumstances today. We use different coins or pieces of paper to count our money and we may not need to build a magnificent house for God, but the principle of self first, or material things before God, is just the same.

4. Pay great attention to the main verbs

This may sound an obvious piece of advice that is quite

elementary from the viewpoint of grammar, but it is amazing how little it is practised.

5. Pay great attention to the symbolism of the prophets

In addition, there is a very common feature in the prophets which does not appear so often in other passages of Scripture, and that is symbolism. Here a good imagination is a great help, not to invent, but to see into a symbol. Ezekiel was told that his ministry would be opposed and be uncomfortable. The Lord said, 'Though briars and thorns are with you and you sit upon scorpions. . . ' No one who has ever walked through the jungle needs too much imagination to know what the Lord meant by briars and thorns being constant companions, and no one who has been bitten by a scorpion will want to sit on one! Ezekiel and John were both told to eat books. What better picture could there be for reading, marking, learning and inwardly digesting a book and making it part of yourself? Jeremiah was sent to the pottery to see a vessel that was spoilt in the hand of the potter and to learn that God can take spoilt human clay and make another vessel out of it.

Sometimes, of course, the prophets do look into the future, and there we must be very careful in defining what is intended as symbol and what is intended as fact. Commentators are divided, for instance, over the question whether the temple that Ezekiel sees towards the end of his book is ever going to be built. Some feel that it is symbolic of the ideal community and point to the picture of the new Jerusalem in Revelation. Others feel that this temple will in fact be built in Israel one day. Obviously each man has to be persuaded in his own mind, but I suggest that in our preaching we should hesitate to be dogmatic on such points. Jehovah's Witnesses have gone astray on a point of symbolism by taking the 144,000 who are sealed as being a literal number. Much of the symbolism of the prophets, however, is simply picture language to bring home a point forcibly.

Practical application

Let us now look at a passage from Hosea and treat it in the same way as previously, writing out the passage to help our understanding. The passage is chapter 14: 1-7 and is part of a book addressed to the northern kingdom of Israel, who had been enjoying a period of great prosperity, but who morally and religiously had gone far astray. Their sins had been portrayed very clearly and God's love had been shown by an acted parable in which Hosea himself married a woman of loose morals and even bought her back from the slave market as a picture of the love of God for his people.

Analysis of Hosea 14:1-7

v.1	Return, O Israel	invitation to repent
	to the Lord your God	come back to the Lord
	for you have stumbled	
	because of your iniquity	sin causes falling
	Take with you words, and	confession needed
	return to the Lord	
	say to Him, 'Take away all iniquity	ask Him to forgive
	accept that which is good and	dedicate yourself anew
	we will render the fruit of our lips	promise right offerings
v.3	Assyria shall not save us	renounce political answers
	we shall not ride upon horses	renounce reliance on military might
	we will say no more "Our God" to the work of our	renounce idolatry

hands	
in Thee the orphan finds mercy'	put your trust in God
v.4 I will heal their faithlessness	God speaks in promise
I will love them freely	cf. Hosea's marriage. We do not deserve God's love.
for my anger has turned from them	
v.5 I will be as the dew to Israel	symbolism of water in a dry country
he shall blossom as the lily	beauty
he shall strike roots as the poplar	strength
v.6 his shoots shall spread out	extensions and growth
his beauty shall be like the olive	attractiveness
his fragrance like Lebanon	refreshment
v.7 They shall return	
and dwell beneath my shadow	God's protection
they shall flourish as a garden	God's cultivation
they shall blossom as the vine	fruitfulness
their fragrance shall be like the wine of Lebanon	refreshment again.

An interpretation

This passage is clearly one about the nature and fruits of true repentance. A people who had rejected their God and gone right away from Him were invited to return and promised wonderful blessings if they did so. I would therefore preach on such a passage in accordance with an outline like the one below. Before I set that out, please notice the symbolism that runs right through the whole passage. Not only is it there in such obvious parallels as the beauty of the lily, but also in a sentence like: 'Assyria shall not save us.' One of Israel's frequent sins was trusting in political scheming instead of in the

power of God and it led her into continual trouble
with her neighbours. Likewise, the reference to riding
on horses was a clear reference to military power, for
the horse was the most important item of military
equipment.

Subject: The need and the promise of revival

1. The invitation to repent

There can be no revival without repentance.
The Lord here issues an invitation to return and come
back to Him.
He also defines what true repentance is.
True repentance involves:

> returning to the Lord whom we have forsaken;
> acknowledging the cause of our troubles in our sin;
> confessing with words and in detail what we have
> done:
>> we ask Him to remove all sin;
>> we rededicate ourselves to His service;
>> we offer to give what we have not been giving as
>> we should;
>> we confess our errors one by one (in their case
>> political scheming, relying on military power
>> and idolatry. In our case maybe planning our
>> own lives, relying on the help of some impor-
>> tant person, or putting someone else in the
>> place of God);
> throwing ourselves on the mercy of God as the
> Father of the fatherless.

2. The promise to restore

When the people of God do in fact return like this, then
God promises to meet them. He promises to heal their

faithlessness. We always worry about the past but God promises to heal where we have let him down.

To love them freely, just as Hosea married and loved his unfaithful wife. We know, too that though the love is free to us, God turned away His anger only through the cross.

To be like the dew: this provides moisture in a dry season.

> It keeps plants alive and comes down daily.
>
> It does not make a noise but its effects are seen.
>
> In promising this, God promises to restore to damaged lives beauty, strength, growth, attractiveness, refreshment.

Under God's protection and cultivation His people will again be fruitful and attractive to others.

Application

Why do we stay away from God so long when He is so gracious in His promises? He has told us what to do; let us do it and claim His promise.

Once again these notes are just the bare bones of what I would normally have written down, but I have set them down here to illustrate how the writing out of the passage can help in the preparation of a message that comes straight from the Word of God itself. The prophets are the most wonderful writings, but they are also very much neglected in the church today.

Study questions

1. Analyse Ezekiel 2:8 − 3:11 and outline a message on the responsibilities and privilege of the minister of the Word of God.

2. What is the meaning of the symbols in Isaiah 40:

1-11, Daniel 7:19-22 and the following symbols in Jeremiah 17: v.1, a pen of iron, a point of diamond, engraved on the horns of their altars; v.6, a shrub in a desert; v.11, the partridge that gathers a brood which she did not hatch?

3. Write down modern equivalents for the symbols expressed by Jeremiah 17 in number 2 above in terms a city dweller would understand.

9

The introduction

Definition

The introduction to a sermon is the means by which the thoughts of the hearers are brought into line with the thoughts of the speaker in the shortest possible time. When you stand up to speak, the mind of each hearer is filled with all kinds of thoughts, ranging from wondering if she has enough food for the next meal to worrying how he is going to repay some debt. However, people do not know what you are going to speak about and are therefore curious for a moment to find out. This is your opportunity to gain entrance, to fasten on that moment of curiosity and to lead your hearers to think what you want them to think. Gain their attention now, and you may keep them for the whole message, lose their attention now, and you will probably never get it back again. Attentive faces are no guarantee of attentive minds. Children let us know when they are bored because they fidget and look all over the place, but adults have learnt to hide their feelings and to look interested when in fact their thoughts are thousands of miles away. Nor can you assume that all of your hearers want to be led in the direction of your thoughts. Some of them no doubt are anxious to hear the Word of God, but others are only casually interested, and others not at all. You have to lead them from what concerns them now to what you want them to think about, and that may be something that has never before concerned them.

It is at this point that the earlier part of the service is so important. If men's minds have been moved by the worship to turn their thoughts towards God, they are much more likely to hear what His Word has to say. True worship not only glorifies God, but prepares men to hear His truth. I have preached in churches where I felt as though I hardly needed to say anything at all. God was so obviously present with us that when I stood up to speak I felt that half of my work had already been done for me. I have also preached in churches where the first half of the message has been spent in a tough battle to gain entrance into the minds of the congregation who were obviously completely unprepared by the worship to listen to the Word of God, and quite unused to giving their minds to the sermon.

Thorough preparation is a must

A good introduction is therefore one of the key parts of a sermon and the preparation given to it may mean the difference between success and failure in communication. A good introduction will be relevant both to the hearers' circumstances and to the theme of the sermon. You may be thrilled with the theme of your sermon, but as yet no one else is; so you have to begin where people are and move them on from there. Again, you may be wonderfully relevant to the circumstances of the hearers, but if you do not link them up with your theme, you will lose them immediately your introduction is over. A bridge has to have foundations on both sides of the gap. If you begin by saying, 'The church in Philippi was founded on Paul's second missionary journey in A.D. 53. . . ', some people will not be listening by the time you get to your second sentence. A.D. 53 to them is so far in the past that you have already made clear to them that what you have to say has nothing to do with their everyday lives. Similarly, to begin by stating the obvious is to invite inattention. 'Today is Christmas Day,' neither informs nor inspires. Nor does it help if you use long words to state the obvious. I once heard a famous speaker begin by saying, 'We all live in a thoroughly contemporary situation.' That sounds very learned but when you put it in plain and simple terms it really means: 'We are all alive now!' Sometimes you may be tempted to make use of a story you have heard, that has impressed you as a good story, that would certainly get people's attention. But if the story has nothing to do with the theme of your message for that day you are wasting your time, for you still have to build your bridge at the other side of the gap and valuable time has been used to no purpose. In fact a good introduction is more than a bridge, for a bridge can be used or not at the user's wish, but a good intro-duction compels your hearers to come with you in spite of themselves. It plays the role of a baited hook in fishing.

Characteristics of a good introduction

1. Arrests attention

The medicine seller in the market knows just how to do this. He knows that most of his potential customers will walk right past him unless he does something to stop them. You and I have to do the same and need to be just as sceptical, about our hearers' desire to listen to us, as he is.

2. Moves from the known to the unknown

There is real movement and, the farther away from the normal experience of the congregation the idea in the mind of the speaker is, the harder it is to bring the congregation all the way. Some messages need little introduction because their theme lies close to the experience of the people, but others need much more careful introduction either because of the difficulty of the subject, or the lack of experience of the hearers. Whatever the circumstances, the introduction must be seen to move from the known to the unknown.

3. Introduces the message briefly and clearly

Some introductions are almost another sermon in themselves, or the preacher gets so carried away with a wonderful story and all its details that when he eventually reaches his message it is rather an anticlimax and the congregation falls back into sleepiness. Introductions are meant to introduce and not to draw attention to themselves.

4. Presents a varied approach to the message

Do not always begin with a story. Do not always begin with a proverb. Do not always begin with a dramatic situation. Once a congregation feels that the preacher has a favourite way of introducing his message, they will know what to expect and the important sense of curiosity will be lacking.

5. Serves the theme of the message

Introductions should not be so dramatic that the rest of the message is dull by comparison. They must be very carefully prepared and thought out, and because they are to serve the main theme they should usually be

prepared last of all. How can you prepare an introduction to a message if you are not sure exactly what
that message will have as its main thrust?

6. Introduces a justifiable and valid message

To lead people to expect that you are going to answer
the whole problem of pain in one sermon is to ask for
people to go away disappointed. Pure honesty requires
that the Christian does not claim more for his message
than he intends to put into it, so, in trying to catch
attention with your introduction, you must be careful
not to carry things too far and claim for what you are
about to say more than is justified.

Types of sermon introduction

Let us now consider different ways in which a sermon
can be introduced.

1. Illustrations

Use an illustration that is familiar to the hearer's experience and apply it to the topic in hand. Jesus began to
speak to the fishermen who had just caught a most
wonderful haul of fish by saying to them, 'Follow me,
and I will make you fishers of men.' There was enough
of the familiar in this to make such a saying perfectly
easy to understand, but also enough of the unknown to
make the disciples want to know more. How could they
become fishers of men, and what did fishing for men
mean in any case? So Jesus used a simple sentence to
fasten the disciples' attention upon Him. Paul, when
preaching in Athens, took hold of the current religious
situation. He said (in Acts 17:22), 'Men of Athens, I per-
ceive that you are very religious. . . . ' He complimented
his hearers on their attention to the matter of knowing

God and then pointed out that he had come to tell them about the 'unknown God' to whom they had built an altar. The King James Version does not give the right sense to modern ears here, when Paul is quoted as saying that the Athenians were very superstitious. You do not attract the attention of the hearers in the right way by suggesting that they are very superstitious, but that was not what Paul meant. He took a known fact about Athenian life and used it to introduce the gospel and to introduce it in the context of their own culture.

2. Striking statement.

A sermon can be introduced by a statement that causes surprise. Jesus said in Mark 2:5, 'Son, your sins are forgiven. . . .' Immediately the whole house full of people wanted an explanation; all were on their toes to hear and see what would come next. This was an outrageous statement and demanded an explanation. Obviously this kind of introduction has to be handled with care lest it be so surprising that it raises hopes that cannot be justified or proves to be untrue.

3. Proverb

Most languages have plenty of proverbs or pithy sayings. Where the listeners know these proverbs and where they form an important part of a culture, they can be used with great effect to gain interest. Jesus often quoted contemporary proverbs, not only in introductions, but at other times too. Part of Jeremiah's introduction to the glories of the new covenant in Jeremiah 31:29,30 takes a common saying that, 'The fathers have eaten sour grapes and the children's teeth are set on edge,' as a jumping-off ground for introducing personal responsibility and the grace of God to sinners in the coming new age.

4. Questions

Even a question can be used for the introduction, provided that it really creates interest. In Mark 2:19 Jesus
begins a short message on the need for all things to be
new by the question: 'Can the wedding guests fast while
the bridegroom is with them?' The masterly way in
which the Lord used the ordinary facts of everyday
life to introduce His messages, short or long, is a lesson
to all preachers. Long and involved questions are
obviously not to be used: 'What in your opinion should
be the supreme objective of the life of the Christian, to
the attainment of which he should aim?' Such a
question would make folk not want to listen any more.

5. Narrative

Here you have to be careful that the story is brief and
relevant to the theme. Avoid anything that takes away
from the main message. Some preachers are good at
telling stories and are tempted to make more of the
story than the truth it is meant to illustrate. Jesus was,
of course, the Master Story-teller, but He never wasted
words and always went to the heart of the problem.

6. Dramatic statement

Say something that will make people curious. Jesus used
this method with the woman of Samaria, John 4: 'If
you knew the gift of God, and who it is that is saying to
you, "Give me a drink," you would have asked Him,
and He would have given you living water.' Being human
she could not wait to find out exactly what the gift was
and who Jesus was, and that is exactly what Jesus
wanted to tell her! If you can only make people eager

and anxious to hear what you are wanting to tell them, your battle is won. Children of course respond magnificently to this kind of introduction. A closed box, a covered jar, or simply a closed fist can have them on the edge of their seats wanting to know exactly what is inside, and, if the truth is told, their parents are just as interested.

7. Dramatic action

Dramatic action has similarities to words spoken to make people curious. It forces itself on their attention. This method of introducing a sermon has to be used quite sparingly, for the pulpit is no stage, but very occasionally to do something that wakes the sleepiest member of the congregation with a jolt serves to gain attention. Jesus did it in the synagogue in His home town of Nazareth simply by sitting down. He had come to His home town after the start of His ministry and His reputation was spreading around. When He stood up to read, as any member was entitled to do, people were naturally curious to know what would happen. When, however, He handed back the scroll and sat down you could have cut the atmosphere with a knife. By simply sitting down He was claiming the right to preach, and the whole assembly was bursting to know what this local young man of whom they had heard so much was going to say. The action though simple was dramatic and effective. The story is told of a student who stopped in a London street and pointed up to the top of a tall building where a gospel text was standing out. Soon a crowd of people gathered round to look at the place to which he was pointing. Then, when they had looked at the poster he quietly walked away and left them. Dramatic action can also be matched by a careful and heartfelt reading of the text. Some passages of the Bible are intensely dramatic. Used with care and with careful use of pauses as well as speaking, such passages grip your congregation at once. John 13:30 is a case in point. You could begin a message something like this: '. . . "And it was night." Yes, dark, impenetrable, irreversible night. Night in the street. Night in Judas's soul. "He immediately went out, and it was night." ' Spoken slowly and with feeling, this introduction never fails to grip.

Write your introduction

Because the introduction is such a vital part of the sermon, write out *the exact words you intend to use.* You do not have to feel absolutely bound by them, but those first words are vital to the success of the whole operation and if you are vague in your own mind how you are going to begin, then everyone else will be. If you have words clearly set out in front of you, then even if you begin in a completely unreceptive atmosphere you will have something meaningful to say in those first vital moments.

Above all things, in introducing your message avoid being apologetic. I always remember a certain bishop in England who would usually begin any talk by saying, 'Of course, I really don't know why you people should be listening to someone like me.' From then on everyone took him at his word and stopped listening. Peter exhorts us, 'If any man speak, let him speak as the oracles of God.' The humility of the messenger is not meant to be a false one and you are, after all, the messenger of the Almighty. It is His Word you bring and that requires no apology.

Study questions

1. Prepare introductions to the messages on the widow's mite, on Hosea 14 and on Psalm 19 included in this book.
2. How were the following messages introduced: Acts 2, Peter's sermon on the Day of Pentecost; Mark 10: 23-31, Jesus' message on the cost of discipleship; Acts 22, Paul's message to the hostile crowd?
3. Note down the way five messages you hear are introduced and later ask yourself:
   a. Was the introduction effective in gaining your interest?
   b. What different ways were used?
   c. Were they too long or too short?
   d. Did they effectively link the experiences of the hearers with the message of the speaker?

10

Illustrations

Chambers' Dictionary defines the verb 'to illustrate' as 'to make bright, to adorn. . . to make clear to the mind, to explain and adorn with pictures'. Sermon illustrations should do just these things. They should bring fresh light and brightness into the message, make the truth clearer to the mind, and enable the hearer to picture in plain terms something that may be quite difficult to understand. They are not the message; they illustrate the message. You have to be careful in case your illustrations run away with you and become the main point of the sermon. People will very often remember good illustrations, but if they only remember those, and not the truth they were meant to illustrate, you will have failed.

Important pointers

When using an illustration check these important points:

1. Know what an illustration is meant to clarify!

If you forget it half-way through, your congregation are not going to receive more light. This, of course, means that you must be thoroughly familiar with the illustration, and not suddenly pick on it because you heard someone else tell a good story. Illustrations need as much preparation as any other part of the message, although that does not mean you should be afraid of introducing one that has just come into your mind if you are sure of the facts and that it will really illustrate your point.

2. Use an illustration to highlight just one thing

If you use the one illustration to point to half a dozen lessons, the chances are that your hearers will either be muddled or bored by the time you reach the end. Let me illustrate from the use of a slide transparency, which, after all, is a picture in the terms of the dictionary definition. A person who really knows how to use a slide will keep it on the screen for a very short time, just a few seconds. He will let the picture tell its own story and will not need to explain: 'I put this slide on to show you that tiny building in the back there behind all those people; you cannot see it very well, but that is where we live.' If he needs to do that he might as well have never shown the slide. Again, some people will keep the slide on for a very long time and describe for you every small detail all over the picture. This defeats the whole object of showing it in the first place. When Jesus spoke His parables, He had one main object in view, and He did not need to explain it for men to get the message.

3. Add the illustration to the message

Many times have I sat through enthralling messages by evangelists that went from story to story and had the audience listening to every word, only to find at the end of the message that sin, repentance and sometimes even the cross have scarcely been mentioned and the Scriptures hardly at all. The Word of God applied by the Spirit of God convicts men of sin and turns them to the Saviour. Your illustrations must serve the message, not rule it.

4. Fit your illustration to your audience

Sometimes Western preachers visit Asia or Africa and bring with them wonderful illustrations that in their own culture speak very clearly, but have no meaning for their listeners. If you are speaking to rural people, city illustrations bring little light. On one occasion a visiting missionary was picturing the disciples after the resurrection going out fishing again. She pictured the scene with the moon shining on the water. The trouble was that her hearers were fishermen, and they know that a good fisherman does not go fishing in the moonlight, because the fish are not around for catching then. If you are preaching to people you know well, there should be no problem, but if you are visiting somewhere else it is useful to check your illustrations beforehand.

5. Reduce your illustration to the essentials

In a sense this is the same as emphasizing one point, but it also means cutting out anything in the story or parallel situation that is not strictly relevant to the point you want to make. Once again, a good slide transparency is neither too dark nor too light, and the object you want people to see is clearly the centre of attraction as soon as the slide appears on the screen.

6. Use more illustrations for less interested audiences

This may mean that they are not so well instructed in the faith, or it may mean that their culture is such that they are not used to listening to connected discourses. A man who works in the fields all day is probably very tired by the evening, and his mind does not commonly think in abstract terms. Truth therefore must be made to live before his eyes so that he is drawn to it and can picture it in concrete terms.

7. *Beware of relying on illustrations too much*

Otherwise, there is a danger that, as with the evangelist above, the illustration may crowd out the message. From this angle too you need to beware of the use of humour in messages. A touch of humour can bring home a point very clearly, but you must be able to bring the people back to the point, and sometimes too much humour makes that impossible. While you want to communicate as clearly and effectively as possible, never forget that spiritual effectiveness comes from a living touch with Christ, not from ability to tell good stories.

Sources of illustrations

1. *The Bible itself is one of the best places in which to find illustrations*

God's revelation has always been clothed in actions as well as in words to explain those actions. The redemption of Israel from Egypt is in one sense one long and glorious illustration of man's deliverance from the bondage of sin. God has acted out His message to man in human history, and the Old Testament is a fund of illustrations of New Testament truth. Unfortunately many people do not know their Old Testament, but by using some of the stories from it as illustrations of New Testament doctrines you can make truth clear, and show the relevance of the Old Testament at the same time. Several of the prophets expressed their message in terms of apt illustrations. Jeremiah, for instance, was told to take a girdle or waistcloth that was brand-new and to wear it. Then he was sent to the river Euphrates to hide it in a cleft of a rock. After some time he went back to recover the girdle and found that it was useless. The whole action was God's way of illustrating the judge-

ment that was coming on His people Israel through their
exile (Jeremiah 13:1-7). Amos in his prophecy (Amos 3:
3-8) used a series of illustrations showing that nothing
happens without a prior cause, in pointing out to the
people that when a prophet speaks it is because God has
first told him to do it. He uses two people meeting by
appointment, a lion roaring because of a kill, a bird
falling to the ground because of a snare, and people in
a city fearing because a trumpet has been blown. Even
so, Amos says, when the prophet speaks, God has
spoken to him first, and indeed the prophet has no
choice to but deliver his message.

We probably find Stephen's speech in Acts 7 quite
difficult to understand. So much of it seems to be a
pointless recital of Israel's history. To his hearers, however, Stephen's intention was very clear, for he chose
passages of their history to show how often Israel had
been unwilling to move forward with God, and how
often they had refused to accept their deliverers. In just
the same way, they were refusing to accept the Saviour
from heaven. Stephen's illustrations were so clear that in
the end his hearers wanted to stone him. In 1 Corinthians 10:11 we read, 'Now these things happened to
them as a warning, but they were written down for our
instruction, upon whom the end of the ages has come.'
In other words, the Old Testament is the ideal source of
illustrations for the Christian preacher.

2. History provides another source of illustrations

However, this is one that has to be used with care,
especially in a cross-cultural context. We are all familiar
with our own history, but other people may never have
heard of our heroes or understand why they were
important.

3. Topical events give a much safer source of illustrations

Even in remote areas, the transistor radio abounds these days so that everyone knows what are the main items of news. In the city areas there is good value to be gained from reading the newspaper, for the illustration of something that only happened yesterday comes home with great force.

4. Everyday events of the life of the community

A pastoral visitation will tell many things that will illustrate the truth of different Scriptures, though of course the preacher must be careful not to be too personal in his speaking.

Life is so full of variety, and the same human problems come again and again in so many different ways, that illustrations should not normally be difficult to find when needed. They may occur to you in the course of writing out your sermon, or you may wish to go through the written material afterwards to decide where an illustration could best be used and which one it should be, but let them fit naturally and not be forced.

Illustrations have limitations

One final piece of advice is to remember that the best of illustrations have their limitations. None of them is complete. At best they serve to illustrate, to shed some light. They are not foolproof. When thinking for instance of the Trinity, there is no illustration existing that can possibly light up all the truth, for the truth of God in His innermost being is beyond human analysis anyway. Yet an illustration may serve to make more understandable that which is deeper than all human reason. We might take the illustration of the sun, for instance. When we look at the sun we do not actually see the sun, but the brightness of the sun. If we looked upon the sun itself we should be blinded. In the same way, we cannot see God, though He is real, but we could see Him who 'reflects the glory of God and bears the very stamp of His nature', Jesus Christ, the brightness of His Father's glory. Yet at the same time we speak of feeling the sun on our bodies. What we feel is neither the sun itself, nor the brightness of the sun, but the warmth of the rays of the sun which are invisible. In the same way the Holy Spirit, who is invisible, is yet real to our hearts and by His presence we are made aware of God. Yet the sun that is there and whose brightness we see and whose rays we feel is one sun, not three. Now I have found this illustration very helpful in shedding light on the doctrine of the Trinity, even though there are many ways in which the illustration breaks down, for there are many kinds of analogy with the sun which are not true of the Trinity, quite apart from the fact that the sun is not personal in the first place. The illustration is not foolproof, but used properly it does shed light, it does illustrate.

Study Questions

1. Prepare an illustration to show:
   a. that unseen things are not necessarily unreal;
   b. the meaning of faith in God;
   c. the power of love in human relationships;
   d. the folly of concentrating only on material things.
2. Why do you think Stephen talked about Joseph (Acts 7:9-16), Moses (verses 35-41), and the tabernacle and temple (verses 44-47) when defending himself before the Sanhedrin?
3. In preaching on Ephesians 1:1-10 how would you

illustrate the following: God's love to us before the world began; the free gift we receive as compared with the cost He paid; the riches of His grace lavished upon us?

11

The conclusion

Appeal to the whole man

When God speaks to man He speaks to the whole man, and the preaching of the Word of God should address itself to the whole man, too. When Peter preached the first Christian sermon on the Day of Pentecost he was careful to speak to the *mind*, the *heart* and the *will*. His message was based on clear reasoning. He pointed out that the disciples could not possibly be drunk because it was too early in the day. On the contrary, what the people had seen happening before their eyes was a fulfilment of the Word of God in the prophet Joel. Peter then developed a closely reasoned argument that Jesus of Nazareth was risen from the dead, and the apostles were witnesses to that, and so were the Scriptures. This Jesus, being clearly raised from the dead, had received the gift of the Holy Spirit from the Father and sent Him forth upon His people. Therefore the existence of what the people could see that day was in itself proof that this same Jesus was both Lord of all and the promised Messiah. This was an argument addressed to the mind, and it needed careful following. Our preaching must also be addressed to the minds of men, so that they understand the real basis of that which we preach.

But Peter did not stop there. His sermon struck at the emotions, at the heart of the people. This Jesus, whom

God had so clearly made both Lord and Christ, was the very same Jesus that those same people had crucified. They were morally responsible for the death of the Messiah and the crucifixion and rejection of the Son of God. This was the climax of Peter's sermon, and the effect on his hearers was that they were cut to the heart. Peter was not afraid to move the emotions of men, nor should we be. The moving was based upon truth presented to the mind, but the moving was none the less real. Preaching that never moves the emotions has something wrong with it.

Yet Peter did not end there. In fact the people gave him no choice, for they asked him right away, 'Brethren, what shall we do?' Until the will of man has been moved to do something about what he has understood with his mind and felt in his heart, the work of God is incomplete. Peter then applied his message by urging the people to repent and be baptized in the name of Jesus Christ; they would then receive both the forgiveness of their sins and the gift of the Holy Spirit.

Preaching that simply informs the mind leads to intellectualism. Preaching that only moves the heart leads to emotionalism, and preaching that only affects the will leads to fanaticism. Reason, feeling, will — all three elements must be present in your preaching if it is to be truly biblical. In a sense all three elements must be present throughout your preaching, so that the truth is applied as it is expounded, and yet the concluding part of the sermon is vitally important in gathering together all that has been said so that the mind is clear, the heart warm and the will active to translate God's Word into life. Paul's practice in ministry he described to the Ephesian elders in Acts 20:20,21 as *declaring* what was profitable, *teaching* from house to house, and *testifying* of repentance to God and of faith in our Lord Jesus Christ. The declaration means an announcing, the declaring of the facts of the gospel; the teaching involves explanation of all that those facts involved, and the testifying is exhortation to do something about it in terms of the response of repentance and faith. His ministry would not have been complete without expecting action on the part of his hearers.

Characteristics of an effective conclusion

1. Comprehensive and emphatic

There should be a summary of the teaching of the whole passage, so that everything is seen as a whole and not only summarized but emphasized. The points you have made should be gathered together so that people are reminded of them and see how they link with each other and lead to the conclusion you have stated. Repetition is one of the important parts of good teaching, and if you present your main points over again people are reminded of them and they should be able to go away remembering them. However, it is important that this summary should be a summary and not a repetition of the whole message. That would be tedious and should be unnecessary.

2. Clear and relevant

There should be clear application of the truth proclaimed in terms of the lives of the listeners. The moral and spiritual demands of the truth should be clear, relevant and pressed home, so that no one is in doubt where he/she stands or what is required of him/her. The power of the Holy Spirit was so manifest in Peter's sermon on the Day of Pentecost that the people interrupted him as he reached his climax and asked what they must do. Such things have happened again and again in history in times of revival. On other occasions, the application came as an integral part of the message. If you read Acts 3:16-26 and Acts 13:37-40 you will notice that not only did the apostles offer the benefits of the gospel, but they also warned against rejecting the truth. 'And it shall be that every soul that does not listen to that prophet shall be destroyed from the people,' Peter boldly declared to the people in the temple. Truth not only carries blessing with acceptance, but loss with rejection. Paul likewise said in Pisidian Antioch, 'Beware, therefore, lest there come upon you what is said in the prophets: "Behold you despisers and wonder and perish. . . ".'

3. Short and timely

The conclusion has often been spoilt because the preacher has not quite known how to finish. Because it is important to leave the hearers with the full impact of the message ringing in their ears, it is essential that you keep your conclusion short and not only *know how* to finish but *do* it. Preachers have been divided into two classes, in this respect: those who say 'lastly' and last, and those who say 'finally' and finish. The second kind are much to be preferred. This means that the conclusion needs at least as careful preparation as any other part of the address, and particularly that you know exactly how you will finish. This does not mean that under the guidance of the Holy Spirit you need to be bound to what you have written down and dare not change it, but it does mean that if you are not quite sure how to finish there is a last clear sentence written down in front of you to be used. Otherwise it is very easy to ramble on, because as you listen to yourself, each successive sentence does not seem quite the right one with which to end.

Study questions

1. In Acts 17:22-31 Paul preached to the Athenians. How did he approach their minds, their hearts and their wills? In which order did he tackle them and how much time in relation to the whole was spent on each? What results followed? What can we learn from this?

2. Write a conclusion to a message on Psalm 19 and to one on Hosea 14. If people asked you at the end of the message the question they asked Peter, 'Brethren, what shall we do?' how would you answer them?

3. Study the letters to the seven churches of Revelation and notice in what way they speak to the heart and what has to be done in each case.

12

The primary need

Presence and power of the Holy Spirit

'Our gospel came to you not only in word, but also in power and in the Holy Spirit and with full conviction' (1 Thess. 1:5). Paul, in writing to the Thessalonians, made no idle boast. The Thessalonian church was there to prove his claim. They knew what had happened and so did the whole district round about, for they not only believed his powerful word but preached it themselves all around the province.

Unless our preaching is visited with power and with the Holy Spirit and with much conviction, we are wasting our time. Simply adding another few thousand words to the overloaded air waves does not justify our existence. We are placed in our position as preachers to see lives changed.

Dr. Martin Lloyd-Jones in his excellent book *Preachers and Preaching* distinguishes between the preparation of the sermon and the preaching of it. He points out that both of these activities are essential to success in the right sense. We cannot expect the Holy Spirit to honour our laziness if we prepare poorly. We must make every effort to see that we have learnt all we can from the message ourselves and have thought through how we will present it. Most of this present book is concerned with that preparation.

Yet the act of preaching is just as important as the preparation, and for this we need continual dependence on the presence and power of the Holy Spirit. Not that we can afford to prepare without this presence either, for He is the One to guide us into all truth and these things are spiritually discerned. Indeed our whole business as preachers as far as our ministry to the church of God is concerned can be summed up as follows: 'in words not taught by human wisdom, but taught by the Spirit, interpreting spiritual truths to those who possess the Spirit' (1 Cor. 2:13).

Self-evaluation and prayer

We must not lose sight of the great importance of the actual delivery of the message. If you preach regularly you will no doubt be familiar with the horrible feeling that hits you when a sermon has fallen quite flat. Perhaps you spent hours in preparing that message, and maybe it thrilled your soul right through at that time, but when it came to the preaching you might as well have been talking about the price of fish to a brick wall. Not that we are always the best judge of the effectiveness of our own messages. You may have felt terrible and there may even have been physical reasons why you did, but that does not mean that God has not used your message to speak to some person when they needed it most. On the other hand, you can leave the pulpit feeling thrilled with your own message and having thoroughly enjoyed giving it, only to find that no one else enjoyed it at all. God has His own ways of keeping us humble, and this is one of them. Certainly, the period immediately after the delivery of a sermon is not the time realistically to assess your ministry. Praise at that moment can lead to pride and criticism to despair. So if someone is helping you to improve your presentation, do suggest to them that they make no comments for twenty-four hours. And for yourself, you are too emotionally involved to be able to make any true assessment, so the best thing to do is to commit the message to the Lord for His use and dismiss it from your mind. That, however, is not to suggest that you should not follow that message with prayer later in the day, but then the prayer is centred on the people and not on yourself.

Review for additional thoughts

Once the preparation of a sermon has been completed and put in note form it can be left until near the time of delivery. Then you need to go through it once again, maybe adding a few fresh thoughts as they occur and warming to the theme again yourself. This is absolutely essential. The best preparation served cold is like a curry without the curry powder. Paul exhorted Timothy to 'Take heed to yourself and to your teaching.' The first part of this word of advice is as essential if not more so than the second. If preaching is truth mediated through personality, that personality needs to be under the control of the Holy Spirit.

Free time before preaching

Perhaps I may mention here how difficult we often make it for our preachers by keeping them busy right up until the last moment before the service. Perhaps the minister is expected to be at the door of the church to welcome people, but can no one else do that? More often, we are just so busy that deacons or elders or wardens never have an opportunity to spend a short time quietly with the minister before the service praying for the power of God to come down. How can a man expect to go into the worship of God with his heart fully prepared to deliver the message of God to his people, if he has just had to sort out a tangle in the choir or find a room for a Sunday School teacher who has just arrived? The worship service may help him calm down and gather his thoughts, but that is not what the worship is for. If we want preaching with power in our services we must free the preacher to prepare himself.

Depend on the Holy Spirit

Preaching, then, demands constant dependence on the Holy Spirit, firstly to illuminate your mind to the truth of God, and secondly to empower your own spirit in the time immediately before delivery, but also thirdly during the actual period of speaking. Not that you are meant to be self-conscious as you preach, but rather God-conscious in constant dependence on His power. You cannot open the hearts of men, or convict the sinner. You cannot warm the hearts of the cold, or revive the fallen from their deadness. But God, in His mercy and grace, has wonderfully ordained that, through the foolishness of preaching, men should believe. You never know what He may accomplish, if you are dependent upon Him. Paul described the Corinthian Christians as 'a letter from Christ delivered by us, written not with ink, but with the Spirit of the living God, not on tablets of stone but on tablets of human hearts'. The writer is Christ. The one who makes the mark on the heart is the Holy Spirit. But the preacher delivers the letter that makes all the difference for time and eternity. Part of the thrill of preaching is never knowing what God is going to do that day. Dependence on the Holy Spirit is not only necessary, it is completely rewarding.

A sermon worth repeating?

What about preaching a sermon more than once? Opinions differ widely, but most preachers have little choice but to repeat themselves and someone has said that if it is not worth repeating it is probably not worth preaching once. Yet you must be careful here. You probably have had the experience of preaching a sermon in the morning that proved to be powerful in the hands of God, and then repeating the same message in the evening and expecting the same result, only to be bitterly disappointed. I doubt whether it is ever wise to preach the same message twice in the same day, because if you have really given yourself on the first occasion you have not had sufficient time to recoup that strength for a second journey through the same countryside on the same day. It is rather like an Olympic runner in one of the long races who wins his heat in style only to find that his performance in the final is poor. He gave everything first time. To change the metaphor to one used by the Rev. Alan Stibbs, a man of God much used in exposition, every fresh print from a negative in photography needs to be given more light. You need time to give that fresh light from the Holy Spirit on the old negative of your sermon notes. Never assume that the second time will be easy, or that no preparation will be needed at all. That is a recipe for disaster. But if you do prepare again and allow the Holy Spirit to rekindle the fire in your heart, then the second, third, or tenth time may well be more effective than the first.

Serious responsibility

Effectiveness in bringing the knowledge of God to men

is our aim. We thought at the very beginning of this book of Hosea's judgement that the people's lack of knowledge went right back to the priests' lack of instruction. Those given the responsibility of teaching God's people must answer for their ignorance. Who is sufficient for these things? Ezekiel also underlines the failure of the preachers of his day to have any effect on the moral, religious and social decline of the southern kingdom of Judah. They did plenty of preaching and they used the right terms to describe it. They said, 'Hear the Word of the Lord!' They spoke and claimed the authority of God for their message, but He refused to honour it. God sent Ezekiel to condemn them for they were those 'who prophesy out of their own minds'. They followed their own spirit and had seen nothing! They had spoken falsehood and divined a lie. 'The Lord has not sent them, and yet they expect Him to fulfil their word.' As a result they were described as foxes among ruins, quite unaware of the devastation around them, and knocking pieces off the walls instead of getting down to a repair job (see Ezek. 13: 1-7). So is every preacher who gets his message out of his own mind without dependence upon the Lord who called him, and who simply says what he thinks his people need or want to hear. How can we avoid such a terrible danger? By exposition.

Proclaim God's unchanging Word

When we go back to the Word of God we find what He has said, and indeed what He is always saying, for no word of God is simply spoken and then left. God is still saying what He has always said, whether it be the message of the judgement of God upon a generation like that of Ezekiel, or of the love of God in Christ. Our job as servants of God and of His Word is to translate the principles of His speaking into terms that modern man can understand and obey. Then we can truly say, 'Hear the Word of the Lord!' We did not think it up. We might prefer not to have to say what we find in front of us. Some of our congregation may be offended, and we may find ourselves very unpopular with them or with others who do not like what we say. Yet in faithfulness to God and in a spirit of love we are bound to proclaim the whole truth of God. Only then are we faithful to our calling.

Study questions

1. What is the most important help that a preacher should have in delivering an expository sermon?
2. When is the appropriate time for self-evaluation in order to improve your sermon delivery?
3. Is it advisable to preach a sermon more than once? Why?
4. How can a minister avoid the pitfall of preaching what he thinks his people want to hear?
5. As an expositor, what do you consider as the main task of God's messenger today?

Appendix A

Psalm 19

Notes of study	General revelation
v.1 The heavens are telling the glory of God the firmament proclaims His handiwork	Creation speaks only of *glory* of God's actions
v.2 Day to day *pours forth* speech night to night *declares* knowledge	a) continuous b) information
v.3 There is no speech nor are there words voice is not heard	c) noiseless speech
v.4 Yet their voice *goes out* through all the earth their words to the end of the world	d) universal (cf. Romans 1:20 they are without excuse)
v.5 *in them* He has set a tent for the sun which comes forth *like a bridegroom* and runs its course *like a strong man* with joy	*Illustration* of the sun a) freshness and beauty b) power and joy
v.6 Its rising is from the end of the heavens Its circuit to the end of them there is nothing hid from the heat	c) universal appearance d) universal experience (Christ the Sun of Righteousness)
v.7 The *Law* of the Lord *perfect* — reviving the soul *testimony* of the Lord *sure* — making wise the simple	pattern name for God's Word what it is
v.8 *precepts* of the Lord *right* — rejoicing the heart *commandment* of the Lord	what it does

    pure — enlightening the eyes
v.9 *fear* of the Lord
    clean — endures for ever
    ordinances of the Lord
    true — altogether righteous

v.10 More to be desired than gold even *much fine* gold	a) value
Sweeter also than honey and the honeycomb	b) taste
v.11 Moreover by them also is thy servant *warned*	c) *effect present negative*
in keeping them — great reward	d) *effect future positive*

Personal appropriation

v.12 Who can discern his errors	aware of error
	hidden fault
	present sins
Clear thou me from hidden faults	Word brings conviction
	prayer
	trust
v.13 *Keep back* thy servant from presumptuous sins	fear of failure
Let them not have dominion over me	prayers to
Then shall I be blameless	clear me
and innocent of great	keep me back
transgression	let sin not rule
v.14 Let the words of my mouth	(Two areas where we sin)
the thoughts of my heart	
be acceptable	
in thy sight	His sight not man's
O Lord my rock	a) strength
my redeemer	b) deliverer

Appendix B

Preaching practice — Evaluation Form

Speaker   Date
Type of audience   Purpose
Subject or central theme

Main points:

Introduction:

Relevant   Brief   Arrests attention
Not exaggerated   Moves from known to unknown

Main exposition:

Arises clearly from the passage
Moves to a climax
Clear
Memorable
Compels attention to Scripture by hearers
Relevant to the needs of men

Illustrations:

Number
Clarity
Effectiveness of use
Relative to the audience

Conclusion:

Does it summarize and emphasize   Clarity
Application of truth to hearers   Brevity

General Points:

Poise   Gestures   Habits
Looking at audience   Enthusiasm

Language:

Tone of voice   Volume   Audible

Any other points: